# THE PONY RIDER BOYS IN THE ALKALI; OR, FINDING A KEY TO THE DESERT MAZE

*By*
**FRANK GEE PATCHIN**

# The Pony Rider Boys In The Alkali; Or, Finding a Key to the Desert Maze

*by* **Frank Gee Patchin**

Copyright © 2023

All Rights reserved.
No part of this publication may be reproduced, stored in a retrieval system, or transmitted in any form or by any means, electronic, mechanical, photocopying or Otherwise, without the written permission of the publisher.

The author/editor asserts the moral right to be identified as the author/editor of this work.

ISBN: 978-93-57484-12-1

**Published by**

# DOUBLE 9 BOOKS

2/13-B, Ansari Road, Daryaganj
New Delhi – 110002
info@double9books.com
www.double9books.com
Tel. 011-40042856

This book is under public domain

## ABOUT THE AUTHOR

Frank Gee Patchin (1861-1925) was born in Wayland, New York, United States. was an American writer of children's books. He is known for his famous Battleship Boy series and his Pony Rider Boys series, which have many readers today as well. Patchin has published more than 200 adventure books. Most of them were published under the pen names of Victor Durham and Jessie Graham Flower. He has also written for the Edward Stratemeyer Syndicate.

# CONTENTS

CHAPTER I — THE DESERT'S MYSTIC SPELL ............................................. 7
CHAPTER II — THE FIRST NIGHT IN CAMP ............................................. 16
CHAPTER III — TWISTED BY A TWISTER ................................................ 25
CHAPTER IV — THE CHARGE OF THE LIGHT BRIGADE ................... 33
CHAPTER V — STALKING BIG GAME BY MOONLIGHT ....................... 40
CHAPTER VI — BAGGED BY LUCKY SHOTS ............................................ 46
CHAPTER VII — CHUNKY COMES TO GRIEF ......................................... 51
CHAPTER VIII — NEARLY DROWNED IN AN ALKALI SINK ............ 57
CHAPTER IX — THE BOYS DISCOVER A RIVER ................................... 65
CHAPTER X — A COWBOY TAKES A HEADER ...................................... 70
CHAPTER XI — A PIECE OF HUMAN SANDPAPER .............................. 76
CHAPTER XII — RUNNING DOWN THE TRAIL ..................................... 82
CHAPTER XIII — COYOTES JOIN IN THE CHORUS ............................. 89
CHAPTER XIV — FUN IN THE FOOTHILLS ............................................. 95
CHAPTER XV — BUD PROMISES SOME EXCITEMENT ..................... 101
CHAPTER XVI — THE BATTLE OF THE STALLIONS ......................... 106
CHAPTER XVII — ON A WILD-HORSE HUNT ...................................... 114
CHAPTER XVIII — ROPED BY ROUGH RIDERS .................................. 121
CHAPTER XIX — WINNING THEIR REWARD ...................................... 127
CHAPTER XX — VISITED BY A HALO ..................................................... 133
CHAPTER XXI — OFF ON A DRY TRAIL ................................................. 141
CHAPTER XXII — IN THE HERMIT'S CAVE .......................................... 146
CHAPTER XXIII — LOST IN THE DESERT MAZE ................................ 153
CHAPTER XXIV — CONCLUSION .............................................................. 158

# CHAPTER I
# THE DESERT'S MYSTIC SPELL

"If this is the desert, then I think I prefer mountains," decided Stacy Brown.

"It is not the desert. We have not reached it yet. This is the Diamond Range," replied Tom Parry, who was to guide the Pony Rider Boys across the great Nevada Desert. "We shall soon be there, however."

"You'll know the place when you see it, Chunky," said Ned Rector.

"And feel it, too, I guess," added Tad Butler under his breath.

"We have the desert on each side of us now," continued the guide. "Were you to fire a rifle to the right or left, your bullet would fall on the baking alkali of the desert."

"Then, if we're so near, why not get out in the open, instead of floundering through these hills?" questioned Stacy.

"I'm thinking you'll wish you were back in the hills before many days," laughed the guide.

"Mr. Parry has his own reasons for following this trail, Master Stacy," interposed Professor Zepplin. "We are entirely in his hands and it is not for us to question the wisdom of his decision."

The guide nodded.

Parry was a splendid type of the plainsman of the great West. Tall, straight, clear-eyed, his bronzed cheeks fairly glistening in the sunlight, he would have attracted attention anywhere. At present, he sat on his pony motionless, the broad sombrero tilted upward above his forehead as he peered into the amber haze that hung over the western horizon.

"Yes, we shall reach the desert soon enough. We are heading for the Newark Valley now, and should be there in time to make camp this afternoon, providing the weather is satisfactory," announced Parry, more to himself than to the others.

"Weather—weather?" stammered Professor Zepplin. "What's the matter with the weather?"

"One hundred in the shade. Isn't that matter enough?" grunted Stacy.

"How do you know, Chunky? You haven't seen any shade to-day," demanded Ned Rector. "There isn't a patch of shade as large as a man's hand in this whole country, so far as I have been able to observe."

"And still less in the country we are about to enter," added the guide.

Tad Butler, however, had been observing the guide keenly. Though the lad had asked no questions, he had caught a note of anxiety in the tone, as well as in the apprehensive glances that Parry kept continually casting to the westward. The guide, catching Tad's inquiring look, smiled and nodded.

"You should always keep your eyes on the weather in this country, especially when on the alkali," he told the boy after the party had started on again.

"Why more there than elsewhere, Mr. Parry?"

"Because storms here are frequently attended with no little peril. You'll see some of them, no doubt, before we reach the end of our journey, and you will wish you hadn't."

"But there's no sign of storm now," protested Tad.

"Perhaps not to you, young man. Do you see that haze settling down like a fog on the western horizon?"

"Yes, I've been looking at it—a golden fog."

The guide smiled grimly.

"I wouldn't call it exactly golden. I should call it fiery," said the guide.

"Has it any particular meaning?"

"May mean most anything. Means storm of some kind—perhaps rain, and maybe wind. If it passes, we'll drop out of here and make camp on the desert to-night."

"That will be fine," said Tad. "We are all crazy for the desert. Since we started out on our trips, last spring, we have experienced almost everything that could happen to us on mountain and plain— —"

"But not including the desert?"

"No."

"You'll find it different; very different."

"I suppose you know every foot of it—in fact its every mood, do you not?" questioned Tad.

The guide, for the moment lost in thought, finally turned to the lad again.

"Moods, did you say? Well, that describes it. The desert is as moody as an old hen with a brood of chickens. Know the Nevada Desert? Sometimes I think I do; then again, I know I don't."

"But you could not get lost— —"

"I have," smiled the guide. "I've been wandering about the alkali for days without being able to find my way back. If you are able to read trails and the droop of the scattering sage brush you will have made a long stride toward knowing your way about the desert."

"I don't understand," wondered the lad.

"No; of course not. It's a long story, but when we have time I will initiate you into the mysteries of reading the desert signs. The west is clearing up. That's good," the guide exclaimed in a relieved tone.

"Which means that we go on?"

"Yes."

"Are we turning off into the desert, did you say?" asked Walter Perkins, with sparkling eyes.

"Well, not just yet, Master Walter. We shall have to refill our water-bags before leaving the range. I take it, you boys would not care to be without water?"

"No, I guess not. But where are you going to get it?" asked Ned.

"About a mile further on there should be a mountain stream. There will not be much water in it just now, but we shall be able to fill our bags and water the stock, I guess."

"Hooray!" shouted the boys.

"The call of the desert is stronger than ever," averred Tad.

"You are not the first ones who have felt that way, young man. 'The call of the desert,' as you put it, has lured many a poor victim to his death. Water is the all important thing when on a journey of this kind, and we shall have to be vigilant that we do not allow ourselves to be without it."

As the guide had said, the stream, when they finally came up with it more than two hours later, was a mere rivulet.

"Call that a stream?" sniffed Stacy.

"No, it's a freshet," replied Ned Rector. "You might take a swim in it were it not for the danger of drowning."

"How are we going to get any water unless we dip it up with a spoon?" asked Tad.

"I'll show you," smiled the guide, dismounting.

Already the stock had sniffed the presence of water, even though there was so little of it. The ponies chafed at their bits and snorted, while the burros of the pack train tossed their heads in their impatience.

"I used to have a plaything that worked just like the heads of those lazy burros," Stacy informed his companions wisely.

"That's about your gait," growled Ned.

"You didn't think so when he saved our lives in the Ruby Mountain," reminded Tad.

"That's right, Ned," confirmed Walter. "Don't be ungrateful for small favors."

"I apologize, Master Chunky," announced Ned, removing his sombrero and unbending in a ceremonious bow to the fat boy.

"We will now make a water hole. Come along if you wish to know how it is done," called the guide.

Leading the ponies and pack animals down along the slender water course until they had reached a natural pocket, the guide halted. With a rubber blanket he formed a basin in the depression in the rocks through which the water had been trickling and losing itself far down in the earth. Two of the Pony Rider Boys held the blanket in place while it was slowly filling with water.

"Now, Master Stacy, if you will be good enough to fetch one of your pails we will water the stock first."

Stacy did so. To save time, Walter brought another pail, so that this could be filled while his companion was giving the water to one of their animals.

It was a slow process; and, by the time the six ponies and four burros had drunk their fill, something more than an hour had passed. By this time the rubber blanket had been thoroughly cleaned by constant rubbing.

"Bring on the canteens and water-bags," directed Tom Parry. "We'll have water enough to carry us through a few days of desert life, at any rate. Load the burros down."

The animals now having satisfied their thirst were nibbling gingerly at the scant growth of sage brush. It was not a tender morsel at any time, but from that time on they would be obliged to subsist almost entirely on the bitter stuff.

"Have you boys filled up?" asked Tom, looking about. "Better drink enough to last you for the rest of the day. We shall have to use our water sparingly for a time now. Take on a supply while you have the chance."

"How about you, Chunky?" laughed Ned Rector.

"Think I'm a camel?" demanded Stacy, with an air of indignation.

"Now, will you be good, Ned Rector?" laughed Tad.

Even the stolid face of the guide relaxed in a broad smile of amusement.

"Then, if you are all supplied, we had better be on our way. If we are going to camp on the alkali to-night we shall have to make time between this and sundown. It's about three hours high."

With a whoop and a hurrah, the boys swung into their saddles, heading joyously for the Newark Valley and the silent, mysterious desert that in the dim, misty past had been a great inland sea.

Readers of the preceding volumes of this series will recall how the Pony Rider Boys came to spend their summer vacation on horseback, under the guardianship of Walter Perkins' tutor, Professor Zepplin. With a capable mountain guide, their first journey was through the wildest part of the Rocky Mountains, where they met with a series of rousing adventures and hair-breadth escapes—experiences calculated to try the stoutest hearts. It was here that the young explorers hunted big game—here that they discovered a valuable mine that had been the goal of prospectors for many years past.

All this was outlined in the first volume of the series, "THE PONY RIDER BOYS IN THE ROCKIES." In the second volume, "THE PONY RIDER BOYS IN TEXAS," was narrated how the four lads joined in a cattle drive across the plains of Texas, becoming real cowboys. Being by this time well hardened physically, they were able to do men's work in rounding up the stampeding cattle, which led them into many thrilling adventures. It will be recalled, too, how, during a visit to the mysterious church of San Miguel, the Pony Rider Boys solved the veiled riddle of the plains, which marked the end of the most eventful journey of their lives. In the third volume, "THE PONY RIDER BOYS IN MONTANA," we find the plucky lads following the old Custer trail over mountain and plain. It will be remembered how Tad Butler, while chasing a bear that had disturbed their camp, overheard a plot to stampede and slaughter the herd of sheep belonging to a rancher whom they knew; how the lad managed to escape from the men who sought his life; his eventual capture by the Blackfeet Indians, his escape, and the final solving of the mystery of the old Custer trail, during which the boys were in the thick of a battle between cowboys and sheep herders. In the volume preceding the present one the Pony Rider Boys were once more in the saddle in search of further adventure. In "THE PONY RIDER BOYS IN THE OZARKS," they met with a series of disasters and exciting experiences which tested their courage almost to the breaking point. They were beset by a band of robbers, who stole their ponies. Nearly all the party, one by one, was lost in the fastnesses of the Ozark wilderness. It will be recalled how the boys, during a visit to the Red Star Mine, were caught in a wreck far underground; how a car of dynamite exploded, making them prisoners in a rocky tomb, and how, after being rescued by a mountain girl, they discovered the real secret of the Ruby Mountain, narrowly escaping with their lives in doing so. No sooner had they brought this eventful trip to a close than they set out to face the perils of the great, silent desert of Nevada.

They were almost upon it now. Its spell was upon them and the lads fell silent as they waited anxiously for the first sight of the land which they had journeyed so far to gaze upon.

They had not long to wait after leaving the water hole where they had replenished their supply.

The guide at last rode out upon a rocky promontory, where he halted, waiting for the others of the party to come up with him.

"Where's the desert—is that it?" demanded Ned, riding up beside him.

The guide raised his hand in a sweeping gesture.

"The desert lies before you," he answered, his eyes traveling meditatively over the miles of waste and mottled landscape.

A brazen glare lay over the scene, while up from the white alkali flats rose a wave of heat that was suffocating. Old, dried-up water sinks lay white and glistening here and there, framed by vast areas of sage brush, while on beyond in the blue distance lay miles and miles of monotonous, billowing hills and mountains.

"Whew!" gasped Chunky, mopping the perspiration from his brow. "This is somewhat hotter than Chillicothe, Missouri. I wish I had a cake of ice to put under my hat."

"Beautiful! Grand!" murmured Professor Zepplin.

"Reminds me of a Turkish bath I was in once in St. Louis," added Ned.

Tad Butler was silent. He was too profoundly impressed even to speak; and even the guide, familiar as he was with the scene, was silent and thoughtful, too. He understood full well the perils, the pitfalls for the unwary, that lay along the pathway of those who sought to traverse that barren waste.

At last he turned to Professor Zepplin.

"Shall we move?" he asked.

The Professor nodded.

"One of you boys get behind the burros and start them along, please," requested the guide.

Stacy Brown complied gleefully. No more pleasant task could have been assigned to him than that of prodding the lazy pack-bearers.

"Forward!" commanded Tom Parry.

The boys clucked to their ponies.

Not an animal moved.

Surprised, the lads brought their spurs against the flanks that they could feel were trembling a little.

A strange, unlooked for thing occurred.

With whinnies of terror the little animals reared and plunged. Before their puzzled riders could control them every pony in the outfit had whirled suddenly and began plunging along on the back trail.

A chorus of "whoa's" rose from the Pony Rider Boys. Quirt and spur were used freely, and firm hands on the bridle reins quickly checked the sudden rush. By dint of force and persuasion the boys finally succeeded in forcing their mounts back. That is, all had done so save Stacy Brown. His pony was spinning like a top, while Stacy red-faced and perspiring was uttering loud, angry shouts, driving in spur and raining quick, short blows on the animal's rump.

The burros had moved just far enough away to be out of reach of Stacy's plunging animal.

At last it threw itself violently to the ground. Stacy, by a remarkably lively jump, cleared his falling mount, but not a second too soon to save himself from being pinned beneath it.

He sat down on the animal's head, puffing from his exertions. After a minute, during which the other boys laughed so heartily that their own ponies nearly got the better of them again, Stacy rose and began prodding his mount with the end of the quirt, urging it to get up again.

But the pony refused to budge.

"He's 'hog-tied,'" nodded the guide, riding up. "Let him stay there till he gets ready to move. No use trying to hurry the beast. He's too much scared."

"Scared at what?" questioned Stacy, looking up apprehensively.

"Yes; that's what I'd like to know?" agreed Ned. "I don't see anything that looks like a scare."

The guide was looking down at the animal pityingly, Tad thought.

"What are they so frightened at, Mr. Parry?" asked the lad.

"My boy, they are afraid of the desert," replied the guide solemnly.

# CHAPTER II
# THE FIRST NIGHT IN CAMP

"The desert?" the Pony Riders gasped in chorus.

"Yes. It is not an uncommon thing. They seem to realize instinctively that there is danger off there. Even in animals that never have been near the desert you will find the same inborn dread of the alkali flats. And I don't know that I blame them any."

"But is my broncho going to lie here all day?" queried Chunky. "If that's his idea I might as well give him another argument that will make him change his mind."

"Let him alone. He'll be better off if you do not force him. When he gets up be gentle but firm with him."

"That's the strangest thing I ever saw," said Tad quietly.

"Most remarkable," agreed the Professor.

The faces of the boys were serious. They too began to perceive the feeling that had stirred the ponies to resist when turned toward the silent plains that lay spread for mile upon mile before them.

After a few minutes Stacy's pony scrambled to its feet. The lad was in the saddle in a twinkling.

"Now, I guess you'll go where I want you to. Whoa! Quit that b-b-b-b-bucking."

The animal had gone into a series of jolting bucks, with back arched and head well down. The fat boy held his seat well. His face was red and streaked with perspiration which ran down it in tiny rivulets under the violent exercise to which he had just been subjected.

The boys forgot the serious side of the incident in their enjoyment of their companion's discomfiture.

Tom Parry gazed upon the scene with more than ordinary curiosity. It was the first opportunity he had had of observing a Pony Rider Boy in action. At that moment Stacy Brown was most distinctly in action. Most of the time there was a broad patch of daylight under him, and when he hit the saddle it was with a jolt that seemed as if it must jar his head from his body.

"Put some salt on his tail," suggested Ned Rector.

"Y-y-y-you do it," gasped Chunky, which brought a roar of laughter from the whole party.

"Yes, why don't you?" teased Tad. "It's the only way you can make good."

"Salting down horse is not my business," laughed Ned.

All at once the pony whirled, heading down the mountain side with a disconcerting rush that nearly brought disaster upon its rider.

With a shout the rest of the boys urged their mounts into a jog-trot and followed on down the trail as fast as they dared, for the descent was steep and dangerous.

"He'll break his neck!" cried the Professor.

"After that bucking I'm sure Chunky's neck is too well fastened to come off," laughed Tad.

Stacy was out of sight. They could hear him yelling at his broncho, so they knew he was still in the saddle and right side up. The other ponies, apparently having forgotten their fear, were following the leader willingly now.

All at once they saw lad and mount burst into view on the plain below.

"He's on the desert!" shouted Tad.

Laughing and shouting words of encouragement to the fat boy, the Pony Riders hastened to the base of the hill. Stacy Brown was still busily engaged trying to subdue his pony, though some of the lads shrewdly suspected that their companion was urging the animal on in order to show off his horsemanship.

In a moment more they, too, were in difficulties. No sooner had their bronchos set foot on the desert than a sudden panic once more possessed them. Professor Zepplin's pony whirled on its haunches, then began climbing the rocks, with the agility of a squirrel.

The others, however, had troubles of their own, which saved the Professor from being laughed at. The animals seemed determined not to be forced to go on, and it required severe measures to induce them to take up the desert trail. Tom Parry's mount did not exhibit the same fear as did the others. Still, it gave him more or less trouble, appearing to be excited, in spite of itself, by the actions of its companions.

At last they succeeded in lining the animals up in an orderly formation. Their next move was to get the burros moving along ahead of them. The way being open and level there was no necessity for leading the pack animals now. These could take care of themselves without danger to the outfit.

"And this is the desert!" marveled the Professor.

"It is," smiled the guide.

"Looks to me more like a landscape of German measles," averred Stacy, as they moved along through scattering sage brush and open sandy stretches.

Now that they had reached the plain itself, they discovered that it was not one level stretch of land. Instead, the country was rolling; here and there were wide reaches of whitish desert sands and alkali sinks. The atmosphere was like an oven. Not a breath of air was stirring. Already the lads were mopping their brows and fanning their faces with their sombreros, while spots of dark shining moisture on the ponies' sides bore evidence that they, too, felt the baking heat.

"I say, fellows, let's find some shade," called Stacy.

"All right, go ahead and we'll follow," laughed Tad.

"I'll ride up to the top of that knoll and make an observation."

Tom Parry smiled appreciatively as the lad galloped up the sharp rise of ground, where Chunky sat on his pony, shading his eyes as he gazed off over the cheerless desert.

"Well, how about that shade?" shouted Ned.

Stacy turned disconsolately and rode back to his companions.

"There isn't any," he said.

"Of course not," laughed Ned.

"But I know how to make some," added the fat boy.

Slipping from his pony he cut some sage brush, which he fashioned about his head in the shape of a hood, so that it gave his perspiring face some protection from the intense glare of the sun.

"Now, all you need is a strip of mosquito netting," suggested Walter.

"And a little red rocking chair," added Ned.

"With a dish of ice cream," laughed Tad.

"I guess you will have to be satisfied with a cup of alkali water," interjected the Professor, dryly.

"You will find the air much cooler, shortly," the guide advised them. "The sun is going down now and I think we had better make camp, if the Professor has no objections."

"Not in the least. In fact, I am quite ready to call it a day's work."

"Where do we camp, Mr. Parry?" asked Tad.

"Right here. It is as good a place as any that we shall find. There is little choice out here."

They were now in a broad valley, the rolling hills covered with a sparse growth of sage brush rising gradually on each side.

The boys threw themselves from their ponies gladly, stripping the saddles from the animals' backs.

"Better stake the animals down, for the first two or three nights, so they won't take French leave," advised the guide.

"How about the burros?" asked Tad.

"Let them roam. They'll stay as long as the ponies are here. The pack animals will fill up on sage, after which they will come back to camp to sleep."

All hands began to unpack. The tents were pitched in record time, cots unfolded and preparations for the night made with a skill that comes from long practice in the open.

"What are we to do for a camp-fire?" asked Walter. "There is not a single stick of wood about here."

"Burn the sage," answered the guide.

"That stuff won't burn," retorted Ned.

"Try it."

They did. In an incredibly short time a hot fire was blazing up, on which they piled armfuls of the stunted desert growth.

"Now, get your food ready and I will cook it," said Parry, as the flames began to die down.

When the fire had settled to a bed of hot ashes Tom thrust the bacon directly into the ashes, placing the coffee pot near the center, around and on top of which he heaped the ashes. It was a new method of preparing a meal, and the lads watched the process with keen interest.

"I shouldn't think that bacon would be fit to eat. However, I presume you know what you are doing," said the Professor.

"It's the only way, sir," replied Parry. "We have to work with the implements that nature has provided."

"Nature must have been in a stingy mood when she made this country," laughed Ned.

"I don't agree with you," said Tad. "It is the most beautiful and interesting scene that I have ever looked upon."

Parry nodded approvingly.

"And as fickle as it is beautiful," added the guide. "The supper will be ready by the time you have the table set, boys."

In spite of the heat the lads realized all at once that their appetites had not suffered. Bacon, jelly and biscuits, which had been warmed over the ashes, seemed to them to have reached the proportions of a banquet.

Stacy helped himself to a large slice of bacon which he proceeded to munch. No sooner had he begun, however, than he made a wry face.

"What's the matter. Isn't the bacon all right?" asked the guide.

"Awful! Somebody's trying to poison me," Chunky shouted, red in the face.

"Must have a brown taste in your mouth,' laughed Ned.

"What's the trouble— —" began the Professor. "Good gracious, there is something the matter with the stuff. Ugh! Never tasted such bitter stuff. Did you purchase this meat in a reliable place, Mr. Parry!"

The guide smiled good-naturedly.

"The bacon is all right, sir. It's the sage brush taint that you get."

"The what?"

"Sage brush. The same taste will be in everything you eat out in this country—that and the alkali."

"Then I starve," announced Stacy, firmly, laying down his fork and folding his arms.

"Any time you starve it'll be because there is nothing to eat," retorted Ned.

"You'll all get used to the taste after you have been out a few days," comforted the guide.

"Never!" shouted Stacy.

"I rather like the peculiar taste," smiled Tad Butler.

"Good as a tonic," spoke up Walter.

Thus encouraged Stacy tried it again, at first nibbling gingerly at the bacon, then attacking it boldly. Even the Professor, after a time, appeared to forget the bitterness of the food, passing his plate for more.

Tom Parry smiled indulgently.

"You'll all like it after a while," he nodded.

"I'm sure I'll have to take back some sage brush with me to flavor my food after we leave the desert," scoffed Ned.

Supper finished the dishes were cleared away, after which the party threw themselves down beside the camp-fire in keen enjoyment of the hour. The evening was delightfully cool, with not a trace of the baking heat of the day.

"Doesn't seem possible that there could be such a change in the temperature in so short a time," marveled the Professor.

"It is the mood of the desert," answered the guide.

"What time do we start in the morning?" interrupted Tad, approaching them at that moment.

"I was just about to suggest that we break camp at daylight, traveling until the sun gets hot. We can then pitch a tent or two during the middle of the day, and rest for a few hours."

"Why not keep on all day?" asked the lad.

"It would prove too great a strain—both on man and beast. At noon we will eat a cold lunch, as too much food in this heat is not good for us. You will find the temperature rising as you get further south, and the hardships increasing in proportion."

"We shall not fall by the wayside," laughed the boy.

"No; I am convinced of that. You lads are as tough as pine knots, but you will need all the endurance you have for this trip."

"If we are going to turn out so early, I think you boys had better go to bed pretty soon," advised the Professor.

"That's why I asked you, sir. I rather thought Mr. Parry would wish to make an early start in the morning. I'll see to the ponies; then I'll go to bed."

"Never mind the ponies. I'll look after them," answered Parry.

"That boy is a splendid type," he continued to the Professor, after Tad had walked away from them to notify his companions of the plans for the morrow.

"They all are," answered the Professor.

"Yes, I have been observing them all day. To tell the truth I was rather doubtful about the wisdom of taking a number of boys across the desert. It's bad enough for men well hardened to the work."

"I trust your apprehension no longer exists," smiled the Professor.

"Not a trace of it left," replied Parry, with a hearty laugh. "Young Brown handled that bucking pony splendidly this afternoon. He's a good horseman for a boy."

"Master Tad is a better one. You'll agree with me if you get an opportunity to see him in any work that's worth while."

"Well, good night, boys," called the Professor, as he saw the lads moving toward their tents.

"Good night, Professor, sleep tight," they shouted merrily altogether. "Good night, Mr. Parry. We'll be up with the birds."

"Birds," sniffed Stacy. "A tough old hen couldn't live out on this desert."

In a short time the camp settled down to sleep. The guide, with a last look about and a long, comprehensive study of the sky, sought his own tent, where in a few moments he, too, was sound asleep.

After a time the moon came up, in the light of which the weather-beaten tents of the Pony Rider Boys were mere specks on the vast expanse of desert.

Not a sound disturbed the quiet scene. However, had any of the occupants of the little tents been awake, they might have observed a thin, fog-like film drifting across the sky from the southwest. On and on it came until finally it had blanketed the moon, casting a veil over the landscape.

Other sheets of film arose from out the southwest, placing layer after layer over the fast fading moon, until finally it was obliterated altogether.

The desert was working out another of its mysterious phases, but none in the camp of the Pony Riders were awake to observe it.

A dense pall of blackness now hovered over the southwest.

All at once a squirming streak of lightning wriggled along the horizon, like a golden serpent, losing itself by a downward plunge into the black abyss beyond the desert.

The air grew suddenly hot and depressing, while a gentle breeze stirred the sage brush on the higher places. The ponies moved restlessly in their sleep, kicking out a foot now and then, as if in protest at some disturbing presence.

Tad Butler, ever on the alert, roused himself, and stepping out in his pajamas took a survey of the heavens.

"I guess we're going to have a storm," he muttered. "I wonder if I ought to wake Mr. Parry? He thought, this afternoon, that there was a storm brewing. Still, there's nothing he can do. The tents are staked down as securely as is possible. No, I guess I'll go back to bed."

The lad did so, and after a few moments of wakefulness, dropped off into a sound sleep.

A few moments later the breeze increased, picking up little patches of sand, which it hurled into the air, scattering the particles over a wide area. Far down to the southwest a low roar might have been heard, and from the blackness there a funnel-shaped cloud detached itself, starting slantingly over the desert. It appeared to be following a northerly course, more or less irregularly, and from its direction, should pass some miles to the westward of the sleeping camp.

Whirling, diving, swooping here and there, lifting great patches of sand and hurling them far up into the clouds, the funnel swept on.

Suddenly, when about three miles to the southwest of the camp, it seemed to pause hesitatingly; and then, as if all at once having descried the little group of tents, started swaying, tottering toward them. As it moved the disturbing roar continued to increase in volume.

Tad Butler heard it now.

He slipped from his tent and stood listening apprehensively.

"I think that means trouble," he said to himself. The hot, oppressive air felt like a blast from an open furnace door. "It's coming this way," he continued.

The lad bounded to the tent of the guide. Slipping inside he laid a hand on Parry's shoulder.

The guide was up like a flash.

"What is it?" he demanded sharply.

"It's I, Tad Butler. I think there is a bad storm coming — —"

"I hear it," snapped Parry, springing from his blankets. He was out in the open in a twinkling, with Tad Butler close upon his heels.

For a moment the guide stood with head inclined, listening intently.

"Bad one, isn't it?" questioned the lad.

"Yes."

"Do you think it is coming this way?"

"I can't be sure. Wait; don't wake them yet," he whispered, raising a restraining hand. "Yes, here it comes! It's a cyclone. Quick, get them out of their tents!"

Almost before the words were out of his mouth the funnel swooped down into the broad sage-sprinkled draw, setting its deadly coils over the camp of the Pony Rider Boys.

# CHAPTER III
## TWISTED BY A TWISTER

"Turn out!" bellowed the guide, his voice faintly heard above the roar of the storm.

"Run for your lives!" piped the shrill voice of Tad Butler.

"Flat on the ground, every one of you!" commanded the guide.

All the warnings had come a few seconds too late. Ere the boys had awakened sufficiently to realize what was wanted of them there sounded above the roar a report like that of a cannon.

The tents were lifted from over the startled Pony Riders and hurled high into the air. A cloud of sand swept over the boys like an avalanche, burying them, suffocating them, while the resistless coils of the funnel picked them out of the drift and cast them far from the spot where but a few minutes before they had been sleeping so peacefully.

Above the roar they heard the shrill voice of Stacy Brown.

"W-o-o-ow!" he shrieked. His voice appeared to be somewhere in the air over their heads.

Blankets, trappings, together with all the other belongings of the party, shot up into the black funnel and disappeared, while the ponies strained at their tethers, floundering, kicking where they had been hurled on their backs, screaming with fright.

The mad medley continued for only a few seconds, though to the unfortunate lads it seemed to have been tumbling them about for hours.

As suddenly as it had appeared the funnel tore itself from the camp and went roaring off into the hills to the northward.

Staggering to his feet, some distance from where he had been caught, the guide rubbed the sand from his eyes and mouth and stood gasping for breath.

An impressive silence had settled over the scene.

"Hallo, the camp!" he shouted when he had cleared his mouth sufficiently to enable him to do so.

"Hello!" answered Tad Butler far to the right.

"Are the others with you?"

"I don't know."

One by one the others of the party straggled to their feet, choking and coughing.

As if to mock them, the moon suddenly burst forth, shedding a brilliant light over the scene which a few moments before had been the center of a whirling, devastating cyclone.

Not a speck of anything save the white, glistening sand of the desert remained to mark the spot where the camp of the Pony Rider Boys had stood.

They gathered shivering in their pajamas, looking fearsomely into each others' eyes, still dazed from the shock and the fright of their experience.

"Wha—what was it?" stammered Walter Perkins.

"A genuine twister," laughed the guide.

"Twister?" questioned the Professor. "Cyclone, you mean?"

"Yes."

"It was awful," breathed Walter.

"All our things gone, too," mourned Ned ruefully.

"You should be thankful that you are alive," chided the Professor.

"How about the ponies?" questioned Walter.

"They're over there. More scared than hurt, I guess."

"But Chunky—where's Chunky? He isn't here!" cried Tad, suddenly realizing that Stacy Brown was not with them.

"Chunky?" wondered the others.

"Why, I thought he was here a moment ago," said Walter in an alarmed tone. "What can have become of him?"

"Probably went up with the twister," suggested Ned.

"Yes, I heard his voice and it seemed to be right over my head," nodded Tad. "We must look for him."

The lads set up a shout as they started running about

"Better look for him that way," directed the guide, motioning in the direction that the funnel had taken after wrecking their camp.

The boys spread out, calling and searching excitedly over the sand, peering into the sage brush and cactus shadows. But not a trace of Stacy Brown did they find, until they had gone some distance from camp.

A faint call at last answered their hail.

"Hooray! We've got him!" shouted Walter.

"Where are you, Chunky?" called Tad, hurrying forward.

"Here."

"Are you all right?"

"No, I'm dead."

The boys could afford to laugh now, and they did, after calling back to the camp that they had found the missing one.

Half buried in a sand drift they located him. Stacy's head and one foot were protruding above the sand, the only parts of his anatomy that were visible above the heap of white sand beneath which he had been buried.

The Pony Riders could not repress a shout when they came up with young Brown and understood his predicament.

"Get me out of here."

"No; you're dead. You stay where you are," retorted Ned.

Tad, however, grasped the foot that was sticking up through the sand, and with a mighty tug hauled Chunky right through the heap, choking, coughing and sputtering angrily, to the accompaniment of roars of laughter from his companions.

Ned grabbed the boy by the collar, shaking him until the sand flew like spray.

"Wake up! Wake up! How did you get here?" demanded Ned.

"I—I don't know. I—I guess I fell in."

"You fell up this time. That's a new trick you've developed. Well, it's safer. You won't get hurt falling up, but look out when you strike the back trail."

"Wha—what happened?" asked the fat boy peevishly.

"Everything," laughed Tad. "We got caught in a cyclone. We don't know whether you were rolled along with it or carried here. Which was it?"

"I guess I flied," decided Stacy humorously. "But I came down so hard that it knocked all the breath out of me. Where's the camp?"

The boys laughed.

"Ask the wind," replied Ned. "We don't know. Come! We'd better be getting back."

"Yee, I reckon there will be plenty for us to do," agreed Tad. "Can you walk all right, Chunky?"

"I guess so."

"Why not fly? It's easier and quicker. Chunky doesn't need a flying machine. He's the original human heavier-than-air-machine," averred Ned.

The guide had by this time gathered a heap of sage brush, to which he touched a match, that they might the better examine their surroundings.

"Anything left?" called Tad, as with his companions he approached the camp.

"I don't see anything but the saddles and the rifles."

"What, everything gone?" demanded Professor Zepplin anxiously.

"It certainly looks that way."

"Where's my pants?" wailed Chunky.

"All 'pants' have gone up," chuckled Ned.

"And so have provisions and everything else so far as I am able to observe," added Tad.

"Then—then we've got to cross the desert in our pajamas," mourned Walter.

They looked at each other questioningly; then the entire party burst out laughing. They were all arrayed in pink night clothes. Not a stitch of clothing beyond these pajamas did any of them have.

"We must look about and see if we can find any of the stuff," decided Parry, his mind turning at once to the practical side of their predicament. "I hope we find the food at least."

"Yes, I'm hungry," spoke up Stacy.

"No wonder, after the shaking up you've had," agreed the Professor. "Guide, where do you think we'll find our belongings?"

"You are lucky if you find them at all. More than likely they are scattered over the Diamond Range for half a dozen miles."

"May—maybe it'll come back and bring our pants," suggested Chunky, at which there was a loud protest.

All hands formed in line, and with the guide to pilot them, started off in their bare feet, hoping to find some of their belongings. Stacy made the first find. He picked up a can of tomatoes. Ned Rector rescued a can of pickled pigs' feet from the shadow of a sage brush, while their guide discovered a sombrero that belonged to Stacy Brown.

But that was all. They traveled nearly to the foot of the mountains, yet not a scrap did they discover beyond what they already had picked up.

"No use going any further," announced the guide.

"Well, this is a fine predicament," decided Professor Zepplin.

"Nice mess," agreed Ned Rector.

"I want my pants," wailed Stacy.

"You'll want more than that. Look at the guide, if you think you are in difficulties," grinned Tad.

All eyes were turned on Tom Parry. Then they uttered a shout that might have been heard far off on the silent desert. The guide was clad only in a blue flannel shirt and a sombrero. He was in an even worse predicament than the party that he was guiding.

Minutes passed before the boys could control their merriment sufficiently to permit a discussion of their situation.

Tom Parry took their joking good-naturedly. He was too old a campaigner to be greatly disturbed over his own laughable condition.

"Something must be done," announced the Professor, after the laughter had subsided. "What do you propose, Mr. Parry?"

"Well, in the first place, like our friend, Master Stacy Brown, I want a pair of pants. I can't very well cross the desert in this rig."

Once more their laughter drowned the voices of the guide and the Professor.

"Is there no town near here where we can get a fresh outfit? I am thankful that I kept my money belt strapped about me. We should be in a tight fix, had I lost the funds, too," said the Professor.

"I have been considering what is best to be done," replied Parry. "I see no other way than that we shall have to ride to Eureka. That is a railroad terminal and quite a town. I am sure we shall be able to get there all we need for our journey. It will prove a little more expensive than in a larger city, however."

"No question of expense just now," answered the Professor. "Will it be necessary for all of us to go?"

"I think it will be best. I don't care to leave any of the party behind. One never can tell what is going to happen, you know."

"So I have observed," commented the Professor dryly.

"How far is Eureka from here?" questioned Tad.

"Between twenty-five and thirty miles. The town lies to the northwest. If it were not for the pack train we could make it quickly, but we shall have to move rather slowly on the burros' account."

"Then why not start at once?" suggested Tad Butler. "The moon is shining brightly and the air is cool. That is, if you can find the way?"

"No trouble about that," grinned Parry. "Your suggestion is a good one. We'll start just as soon as I can get ready."

"I don't see anything left here to get ready," laughed Ned.

"You will excuse me, gentlemen, but there is something that I shall have to get ready," replied the guide with a peculiar smile.

"What's that?" demanded the Professor.

"I've got to take a double reef in my shirt before I can go anywhere, except to bed."

The boys shouted again.

Tom Parry hurried off beyond the ponies, where he was engaged for several minutes. When he returned they discovered that he had taken off his shirt. First he had cut off the sleeves, and by thrusting his feet through the arm holes had made for himself a very substantial pair of trunks. This odd outfit he had made fast about his waist with a thong of leather that he had cut from a bridle rein. This, with the broad-brimmed sombrero, completed his outfit.

The sight was too much for the Pony Rider Boys. They shouted peal after peal of merriment, in which the Professor joined, though in a somewhat more dignified manner.

Tom Parry's mouth was stretched in a grin as he got busy saddling the ponies and urging the sleepy burros to their feet.

"I think we are all ready now," the guide called back to the others.

With many a shout and jest the strange procession started off across the desert, under the brightly shining moon, the cool evening breezes making their scanty covering none too comfortable.

The boys devoted the greater part of their attention to the Professor and Tom Parry, both of whom were riding as dignifiedly as if they were leading a parade at a Fourth of July celebration. Every little while the boys, unable to contain themselves longer, would burst out into merry peals of laughter.

"Hope it doesn't snow," said Stacy Brown wisely.

"No," retorted Ned. "The colors in your pajamas might run."

"That's where the guide has the better of us," retorted Tad a little maliciously, which brought still another laugh from the boys.

"Say, fellows, this saddle is getting harder every minute," called Chunky, who was riding back and forth behind the pack train, urging on the burros.

"Stand up in your stirrups now and then," suggested Tad.

"What, in my bare feet?" yelled the fat boy. "Think I want to get pancake feet?"

"Chunky's getting aristocratic," jeered Ned. "He's so proud of those high insteps of his that he has to take off his shoes every little while to look at his feet. He's afraid they'll cave in some time when he isn't looking."

Daylight came all too soon, and following it the sun burst forth in a blaze of heat. Ahead of them across the desert they were able to make out the town of Eureka.

"Say, Mr. Parry, aren't you afraid this sunlight will spoil your complexion?" called Ned.

The guide grinned good-naturedly.

"Never mind," he retorted. "Your turn will come pretty soon, young man."

Ned Rector did not catch the significance of the remark just then, but he understood a few hours later.

# CHAPTER IV
# THE CHARGE OF THE LIGHT BRIGADE

"You are not going to ride into town in daylight, are you?" demanded Ned in surprise.

Though they had sighted the town of Eureka early in the morning, it was well along in the afternoon before they finally came up with it. Desert distances are deceptive and the further they journeyed the less headway did they seem to be making. This surprised all save the guide.

Parry explained to them that the clear air brought distant objects much closer than they really were.

"We are going into town exactly as we are," replied the guide in answer to Ned's question. "Why not?"

"Well, maybe you are, but I'm not," returned Ned.

"It may improve your complexion, young man," retorted Mr. Parry.

"I'll stay out here and hide on the desert while the rest of you go on in," said Ned.

"No, you don't," shouted the lads all at once. "You go willingly or we carry you."

They gathered around him threateningly.

"If you want a mix-up, we're here," warned Chunky, pushing his pony up beside that of Ned Rector.

Ned, forgetting for the instant that he was in his bare feet, let drive a kick at the side of Stacy's pony.

"Ouch!" roared Ned.

Jerking the injured toe up to the saddle, he grabbed it with both hands, rocking back and forth, for his foot had struck the pony with such violence that it is a wonder every toe on the foot was not broken.

"Did 'oo hurt 'oo little tootsie-wootsies?" cooed Chunky, with a grimace.

Ned Rector, forgetting the pain for the instant, made a quick grab for his tormentor. He just barely reached the sleeve of Chunky's pajamas. But his sudden movement caused the fat boy's pony to leap suddenly to one side.

Ned landed on his head and shoulders in the desert sand, feet kicking the air, to the accompaniment of yells of derision from his companions.

With red face and angry eyes, the lad scrambled to his feet and started limping to his pony, which had sprung to one side, where it stood, evidently wondering what next was about to happen.

"I'll get even with you, Chunky Brown," Ned growled, as he climbed into his saddle.

"Now, now, Ned!" warned the boys. "Take your medicine like a man. Chunky never got mad when you nagged him."

"I'll get even with him. I'll ––"

Tad rode up beside the angry lad.

"Ned, you'll do nothing of the sort," said the boy gently. "You're mad, now, because your toes hurt. When they stop aching your temper will improve at the same time."

"Oh, pshaw! Stop your preaching. Of course it will. I'm a grouch. I take back all I said just now. Chunky, when these toes get straightened out—they're all crooked now—I'll come over and hobnob with you. I deserve all you can give me."

"You bet you do," chorused the lads.

"Stop teasing him," commanded Stacy, with well-feigned indignation. "Can't you see his toes hurt him?"

The incident was lost sight of in the general laugh that followed. The others were beginning to appreciate that Stacy Brown possessed a tongue as sharp as any of them.

Ned now offered no further protest to entering the village, but it was observed that he dropped back behind the others as they reached the outskirts of the town.

Tom Parry and Professor Zepplin were riding ahead, one in pajamas, the other clad in trunks—which resembled a meal sack—a sombrero hat and a sardonic grin of defiance. The others trailed along behind.

Not one of the party glanced to the right or left of him, except Stacy Brown, who could scarcely contain his bubbling spirits.

"They'll think it's some new kind of a menagerie come to town," he confided to Tad, who was riding beside him.

"Then I hope they don't shoot the animals," laughed Tad.

By this time they had entered the main street, down which they rode at a pace that the burros could follow. People passing along the street paused and gazed in unfeigned astonishment at the strange procession which they saw approaching.

The most conspicuous of them all was Tom Parry. He was a sight to behold, but not one whit did he care for the amazed stares that greeted his strange outfit.

Soon the grins of the populace gave place to yells of derision.

"Look at the purty boy with the pink toes there behind," shouted one, pointing to Ned Rector.

Ned's face went crimson.

"Now, aren't you glad you didn't lose the tootsie-wootsies?" teased Chunky.

Ned made no reply, but it boded ill for any of his tormentors who got within reach of his long arms. Already more than a hundred persons had turned to follow the strange outfit. This number was being rapidly added to as they proceeded.

"For goodness' sake, how much further have we to go?" begged Ned.

"The general store is down at the end of the street," the guide informed him. "I presume you want to get some clothes the first thing?"

"I should say so."

A whoop and a yell sounded far down the street.

"Here's trouble," muttered Tad, instantly recognizing the cowboy yell.

A band of them at that instant swung around a corner, straightening out in the main street, letting go a volley of revolver shots into the air. The band had come to town with a shipment of wild horses that had been captured among the desert ranges. They had been in Eureka for twenty-four hours and were by this time ready for whatever might turn up. The horsemen clad in pink pajamas attracted their attention at once. Here was fair game.

"Who-o-o-o-p-e-e-e!"

The shrill cry sent a shiver to the hearts of the boys. It was not a shiver of fear, either.

In a moment more the Pony Rider Boys were the center of a ring of racing ponies, as the horse-hunters dashed round and round, yelling like mad and firing off their revolvers.

"Oh, see that purty boy with the pink toes!" jeered one.

"Give him the tenderfoot dance," yelled another. "He ought to be able to dance the fairy lancers on them pinkies."

Ned did not dare refuse. He slipped from his pony, and, limping to the center of the ring which the racing ponies had formed about them, began to dance as the bullets from the revolvers of the cowboys struck the ground, sending up little clouds of dust under his feet. Faster and faster barked the guns, and faster and faster danced Ned Rector.

Stacy Brown was almost beside himself with joy.

"Better look out, or you'll be doing it next," warned Tad.

Evidently the cowboys had not recognized Tom Parry as yet. He might be the next victim.

Finally Tad rode his pony forward, right through the fire of the skylarking cowboys.

"I guess you've had enough fun with him, fellows," he warned. "Let up now."

A jeering laugh greeted the lad's command. Their attention was instantly turned to him.

"Get off that broncho and give us a dance, young fellow," they shouted.

"Thank you, I'm not dancing to-day," smiled Tad Butler.

"Ain't dancing? We'll see about that. Come off that nag."

Tad shook his head. At that instant a rope squirmed through the air from a moving pony. Butler threw himself to one side just in time to avoid it. The lad's eyes snapped.

"Guess I'll take a hand in this, too," he growled.

The lad unlimbered his rope in a twinkling and let fly at the cowboy who had just sought to rope him. With unerring aim Tad's lariat caught the left hind foot of the cowman's broncho. Pony and rider went down like a flash.

Instantly there was a loud uproar. The horse-hunters yelled with delight; at least all of them save the cowboy who had bit the dust, and he sprang up, bellowing with rage, as he made for the grinning Tad.

Tom Parry decided that it was time for him to take a hand.

The guide jumped his pony between Tad and the angry cowboy.

"That'll do, Bud! You stop right where you are!" Tom commanded.

"But the miserable coyote roped me."

"You tried to rope him first."

"It's Tom Parry," shouted the cowmen. "Hey, Tom! Them's a fine suit of clothes you've got on there. Where'd you get them?"

"Call off Bud and I'll tell you," grinned Tom, "He's got no reason to interfere with my boys here."

Laughing uproariously, the cowboys forced their bronchos between Bud and the others, cutting him off and bidding him attend to his own business. Then the cowmen halted their ponies, after closing in about the Pony Rider Boys, while Tom Parry related the experiences they had passed through on the previous night.

"Come along. We'll take you to a place where you can get all the pants you want," shouted the leader of the party, after Tom had finished his story.

The cowboys wheeled their ponies and the procession moved on down the street. They had discovered that the Pony Rider Boys were not the band of tenderfeet that they had at first taken them for.

Arriving at the store, the lads lost no time in leaping from their ponies, which they tethered at the rail in front, and hurried into the store. This was a postoffice as well as general trading post.

Half the town, it seemed, had gathered outside the building to get a look at the nearly naked strangers who had ridden in a short time before. But once inside the store, the boys did not propose to exhibit themselves further if it were possible to avoid it.

An entire new outfit was necessary—tents, provisions and all, and to purchase all these things would occupy the greater part of the rest of the afternoon.

No sooner had they entered the store and made their wants known, than the boys became conscious of the presence of ladies. The boys could not see them plainly, because it was a dim, dingy place at best.

But, all at once Ned felt a cold chill run down his back. One of the ladies was speaking to him.

"Isn't this Mr. Rector?" asked a pleasant voice. "I am quite sure I am not mistaken."

Ordinarily Ned would have been glad to meet an old acquaintance, but when a boy is clad only in a pair of pink pajamas, his feet bare of covering, he is not particularly anxious to see anyone he knows.

It was so with Ned Rector. At first he pretended not to hear. A hand was placed lightly on his shoulder. Then he turned, his face flushing painfully.

"I am Mrs. Colonel McClure from Texas," she informed him. "We had the pleasure of entertaining you and your companions when you were with the cattle drive in our state."

Ned bowed and mumbled some unintelligible words. He failed to note the twinkle in the eyes of Mrs. McClure.

"And this," she continued, "is my niece Miss Courtenay, Miss Barbara Parks and Miss Long," continued Mrs. McClure mercilessly.

The young women were blushing furiously as they acknowledged the introduction. Ned failed to observe it, however. His eyes were on his feet and the pink toes which seemed abnormally large at that moment.

"Where are your companions, Mr. Rector? I thought they were with you a moment ago?"

"Wh—ye—yes—they are here, they— —"

Ned looked about him blankly. No one was in sight. Then he discovered the grinning face of Stacy Brown peering at him from behind the postoffice wicket.

At the first alarm Walter Perkins had sunk down behind a cracker barrel with Tad Butler crouching behind him. Over behind the counter was the guide, while, behind a pile of horse blankets, Professor Zepplin lay flat on the floor, shrinking himself into as small a space as possible.

Ned Rector was left to face the enemy alone.

# CHAPTER V
# STALKING BIG GAME BY MOONLIGHT

The tension of the moment was relieved by a merry laugh from Mrs. McClure and her friends, in which Ned Rector joined spontaneously. The situation was too funny for even his offended dignity to resist.

The result was an invitation for the entire party to dine with Mrs. McClure and her friends that evening. Ned Rector accepted on the spot, much to the disgust of his companions, who felt a diffidence about meeting the ladies after the exhibition in the store.

However, after they had properly clothed themselves they felt better, and the evening passed at the home of Mrs. McClure's friends was one of the most enjoyable they experienced.

At sunrise next morning the Pony Rider Boys were once more on the desert, bubbling over with spirits and anticipation.

"I've got another invitation for you boys," announced Tom Parry after they had halted for the midday rest.

"I hope we'll have some clothes on when it comes off, then," growled Ned.

"It won't make much difference whether you have or not, so far as this invitation is concerned."

"What is the invitation?" asked Professor Zepplin.

"Bud Thomas and the other cowboys are hunting wild horses for market, you know?" replied the guide.

"Wild horses?" marveled Walter.

"Yes."

"I didn't know there were any about here," said Tad.

"It is estimated that there are all of a hundred thousand wild horses in the different ranges of this state," replied the guide.

"You haven't told us yet what the invitation is," reminded Stacy.

"You haven't given me a chance," laughed Tom. "Well, the invitation is to join in a wild horse hunt."

"Hooray!" shouted the lads.

"Very interesting," agreed the Professor.

"And lively, too," added the guide. "The boys took quite a fancy to you young gentlemen after the roping trick, and said if you would join in a hunt, you'd get all the fun that was coming to you."

Tad grinned at the recollection of their first meeting with the wild horse hunters.

"Whe—when do we join them?" asked Chunky enthusiastically.

"It will be a week or more yet before we reach that part of the desert where the hunts take place—that is, if we have good luck. But if we have any more such experiences as we have just passed through we shall not get there this summer," laughed the guide.

By sunset, that day, the town of Eureka had disappeared behind the copper colored hills, and the Pony Rider Boys were again merely tiny specks on the great Nevada Desert.

They pitched the new white tents for the first time that night, having made camp earlier than usual because they were not accustomed to working with the new outfit. No one knew where to find anything, which furnished the lads with plenty of amusement.

Ned and Tom Parry cooked the supper over a sage brush fire. They had brought a few cans of milk with them, but after sampling it all hands declared their preference for the condensed brand of which they had purchased a liberal supply. The fresh milk procured in Eureka was strong with the sage brush taste, as was almost everything else in that barren country.

The ponies refused the sage brush for their evening meal, having had a supply of real fodder back in town, so they were staked out near a growth of sage that they might browse on during the night should they decide that they were hungry enough.

"Well, I wonder what will happen to-night," said Tad, as they finished the evening meal.

"Let us hope that it will be nothing more serious than pleasant dreams," smiled Professor Zepplin.

"That means you, Chunky," nodded Ned. "You are not to have the nightmare to-night, remember."

"And you look out for your tootsie-wootsies," retorted Chunky.

"We shall have to take a long ride to-morrow," announced the guide.

"Why to-morrow?" asked Ned.

"It is all of twenty miles to the next water hole, or where the next water hole should be. One cannot depend upon anything in this country."

"Haven't we enough water with us?" asked the Professor.

"Enough to last us through to-morrow—that's all. We shall have to get water at night; so, if we have no interruptions during the night, we shall make another early start."

"Stacy, see to it that you do not lose your trousers this time. We don't wish to be disgraced by you again to-morrow," warned Ned.

Stacy merely grimaced, making no reply. He knew that he had not been the one to get the worst of it, and so did his companions. He was quite satisfied with the punishment that had been meted out to Ned Rector.

All hands turned in shortly after dark. They were tired after the long day's ride in the broiling sun. Besides, they had not yet made up the sleep they lost two nights before when the "twister" invaded their camp and wrecked it.

The boys had been asleep only a short time, however, before the entire camp was startled by a long, thrilling wail.

All the Pony Riders were wide awake in an instant, listening for a repetition of the sound. It came a moment later.

"K-i-i-o-o-o-o! K-i-i-o-o-o-o! K-i-i-o-o-o-k-i!"

The boys leaped from their tents. The sound plainly come from some wild animal, but what, they did not know.

"Wha—what is it? A lion?" stammered Stacy.

"I—I don't know," answered Walter. "Do you, Tad?"

"I certainly do not. It's no lion, though. There are none here?"

"Maybe it's a pack of wolves," suggested Ned. "There must be a lot of them to make such a howling as that."

"D-d-d-d-do you thi—thi—think they're going to attack us?" stammered Stacy.

"How do we know?" snorted Ned.

Neither the Professor nor the guide having made their appearance, the boys took for granted that the two men were asleep. Such was the case so far as the Professor was concerned, but Tom Parry was lying on his bed awake, a quiet smile on his face.

"Are you sure it's a wild animal, Tad?" whispered Walter.

"Of course. What else could it be?"

"Then I'll tell you what let's do."

"What?" demanded Ned.

"Let's get our rifles and crawl up to the top of that knoll yonder, where the sound seems to come from— —"

"And take a shot at them," finished Ned. "Good idea. What do you say, Tad?"

"I guess there will be no harm in it," decided the lad, considering the question for a minute.

They had moved away from the tents so that the sound of their voices should not arouse the sleeping men there.

"Two guns will be enough. We're not so liable to hit each other if only two of us have them."

"Who is going to shoot?" demanded Walter.

"What's the matter with Ned and Chunky?"

That suited all concerned.

"You'd better hurry. The animals have stopped howling," advised Tad.

Ned and Stacy ran lightly to their tents, returning quickly with their rifles. Stacy bore the handsome telescope rifle that he had won in a pony race during their exciting trip through the Ozark Mountains. Even in the moonlight one could see a long distance with the aid of the telescope on the gun's barrel.

"See the brutes?" asked Stacy, with bated breath.

"No, nor hear them, either," answered Walter.

"I'll tell you what we'd better do," suggested Tad.

"Yes," answered Ned anxiously.

"We'll crawl along in the shadow to the south. I think the prowlers are up there on the ridge to the west. If they are, they'll be watching the camp-fire. Maybe they have smelled us and run away by this time, even if they didn't hear us talking."

"Keep still, everybody," warned Ned.

The boys stole along as silently as shadows. After moving some ten rods to the south, Tad motioned for them to turn west, which they did.

No sooner had they changed their course, however, than Chunky with a loud "Ouch!" plunged headlong, his rifle falling several feet ahead of him. With frightful howls he began hugging one foot, rocking back and forth in great pain.

"What's the matter?" snapped Ned Rector.

"My foot! My foot!"

"What about it — —"

"I — I don't know. I — —"

Tad grabbed the boy by the collar, jerking him clear of the place. The first thought that came to him was that Stacy had been bitten by a snake, though Tad did not even know whether or not there were snakes on the desert.

"Nice chance we'll have to shoot anything," growled Ned in disgust. "Stop that wailing."

"It hurts, it hurts — —"

"Keep still. I'll find out what the trouble is," warned Tad, dropping down and examining his companion's injured foot.

"Ouch!" exploded Chunky, jerking his foot away.

"If you want me to help you, you'll have to be quiet."

Butler pressed gently on the bottom of the injured foot with the fingers of one hand, the other holding Chunky's ankle in a firm grip.

"Humph!" grunted Tad. "He's stepped on a cactus bush with his bare foot. It's full of prickers. Hold still and I'll pick them out."

"Guess there's no use to keep still any longer. Those animals probably have run away before this," complained Ned.

"K-i-i-o-o-o-o! K-i-i-o-o-o-o! K-i-i-o-o-o-k-i!"

"S-h-h-h!" warned Tad. "They're there yet. Shall I take your rifle, Chunky? You probably don't feel much like tramping up the hill in your bare feet."

"No!" exploded the fat boy. "I guess if there's any shooting to be done, Stacy Brown can do it, even if he's only got one foot to hop along on."

Scrambling to his feet, Stacy recovered his rifle. He had forgotten all about his injured foot now.

Cautiously the boys crawled up to the top of the rise of ground.

"Sit down, everybody," directed Tad. "We ought to be able to see them from here."

Not a thing save clumps of sage brush met peering eyes of the Pony Rider Boys.

"Lay the barrel of your gun over my shoulder and look through the telescope," directed Tad softly.

Pointing the gun to the southward, Stacy rested it on his companion's shoulder, placing an eye to the peep hole. The lads fairly held their breath for a minute.

"I see him! I see him!" whispered Stacy in an excited tone.

"What is it?" demanded Ned. "Where?"

"I don't know. I guess it's a wolf."

"How many?" asked Walter, crawling up to him.

"See only one."

"Take your time, Chunky," cautioned Tad in a low voice. "Draw a careful bead on the fellow and let him have it."

"Over your shoulder?"

"Sure. You never'll hit him without a rest."

Once more they held their breath.

At last Stacy exerted a gentle pressure on the trigger.

There followed a flash and a roar.

"O-u-u-c-h!" yelled the fat boy.

The end of the telescope had kicked him violently in the eye as the gun went off.

# CHAPTER VI
## BAGGED BY LUCKY SHOTS

"K-I-I-O-O-O! K-I-I-I-O-O-O!"

"There he goes!" shouted Walter.

Stacy was picking himself up from the ground where the rifle had kicked him.

Bang!

Ned Rector had risen to his feet the instant Stacy fired. Throwing his rifle to shoulder, he fired at an object that he saw bounding down the opposite side of the hill.

"I got him! I got him!" shouted Ned, dancing about in his glee. "Chunky Brown, you're no good. All you can do with a rifle is to get kicked and fall in. Take a lesson from your Uncle Dudley — —"

"Good shooting, boys," said a laughing voice behind them.

They whirled around and found themselves facing Tom Parry, who had crept up to see that the boys got into no trouble.

"You here?" demanded Tad Butler sharply.

"I am that. Think I could let you boys go off with a couple of guns to hunt wild animals? Not without Tom Parry — no, indeed!"

"I got him, Mr. Parry," glowed Ned. "Did you see me tumble him over?"

The guide nodded good-naturedly.

"And Chunky missed him, even though he had a rest over Tad Butler's shoulder. Chunky can't shoot."

"Yes, I can, too," objected the fat boy.

"We'll see," replied the guide. "I am not sure whether he can shoot or not."

"What do you mean, Mr. Parry!" asked Walter. "Chunky shot at the animal and missed it, didn't he?"

"What kind of an animal was it?" interjected Ned.

"A coyote."

"I thought it was a wolf," muttered Stacy Brown. "How many of them was there?"

"Only one, you ninny. And I shot him," scoffed Ned.

"We'll go down the hill and find the one you got, Master Ned," decided the guide, moving away, followed by the rest of the party.

No sooner had they started than they heard Professor Zepplin, down in the camp, shouting to know what the shooting meant.

"It's all right, Professor," called the guide. "The boys have been shooting up some wild game. You'll be surprised when you see what they got."

Down the hillside sprang the enthusiastic lads.

"Remember, you're all barefooted," warned the guide. "You don't want to pick up any more cactus thorns."

"Were you here then?" demanded Tad, glancing up sharply.

"I was with you from the time you left the camp."

"Here he is," shouted Ned, who had run on ahead of the others in his anxiety to learn the result of his shot. "And I caught him on the wing, too, didn't I?"

"You certainly did."

"Just lift him. He's a whopper," went on the lad enthusiastically. "I'd like to see any of the others in this outfit make a shot like that—"

"Chance shot," mumbled Stacy. "Hit a bird once myself a mile up in the air, but I didn't flap my wings and crow about it. I couldn't have done it again. Neither could you have hit that—that—what do you call it!"

"Coyote," replied the guide, but he pronounced it "kiute."

"Oh, I don't know," grumbled Stacy.

"Suppose we go up the hill now and see what Master Stacy shot," suggested the guide, starting away.

"Shot?" sniffed Ned Rector. "Don't you know what he shot?"

"Yes, we know," interrupted Walter.

"He shot thin air, that's what he did."

"We shall see, we shall see," answered the guide enigmatically.

Though Stacy did not grasp the guide's meaning, he did catch a note in the tone that filled him with hope. Yet Chunky was unable to see how he could have hit anything, in view of the fact that Ned had shot the coyote.

Tom Parry strode up to the crest of the hill and began looking about, peering behind sage bush and greasewood. The boys were a little to the north of him, all hunting for they knew not what. Ned Rector had seated himself by the side of his dead coyote, stroking its rough coat proudly.

A sharp whistle from the guide attracted their attention.

"What is it?" called Tad.

"Come over here. I've got a surprise for you."

The boys obeyed on the run.

Tom Parry stood with a grin on his face, pointing a finger to the ground.

"What is it? What is it?" demanded the lads in chorus.

"Why, it's a dead animal," marveled Walter.

"Then that's what the coyote was doing up here. It was after the meat on the dead one," announced Ned. "I knew there must be some good reason for its remaining so near camp all that time."

"Guess again," sniffed Stacy, who had thrown himself down beside his prize.

"What's that?" asked Tad, who already suspected something of the truth.

"It's my coyote, that's what it is."

Tom Parry nodded.

"He's right. He killed the animal the first shot — —"

"Then — then — —" stammered Ned.

"There were two of them. Master Stacy killed one and you the other, and for your gratification I'll say that they are a very difficult animal to kill. One might try a hundred times and never hit one."

"If one knows how to shoot, it isn't," spoke up Stacy pompously.

"Which you certainly do," laughed the guide.

"May we take them back to camp and skin them?" asked Ned.

"You may take them in, of course; but I would not advise you to skin the brutes. The skins are not worth anything in the first place, and in the second, we should be unable to keep them all the way across the desert, I am afraid."

"You mean they would spoil?" questioned Ned.

"Yes."

"Then we'll take them down to show to the Professor. After that we'll bury them."

"Not necessary at all," smiled the guide. "The buzzards will attend to that part of the work. They'll be around in the morning. You'll see them."

"But how will the buzzards know?" asked Walter.

"That I cannot say. They do know. Instinct, I suppose. All animals and birds have the instinct necessary for their kind, yet it is all a mystery to us."

Very proudly the lads dragged their trophies to camp, where, after heaping fresh sage brush on the fire, the youngsters stretched the carcasses out full length that Professor Zepplin might see.

"Very fine, young men. You say they were howling and woke you up?"

"Yes; didn't you hear them!" answered Stacy loudly.

"Indeed I did not. The first thing I heard was the report of a rifle, and then, in a few seconds, another. I couldn't imagine what was going on. When I tumbled out and found the camp deserted, I was alarmed. I feared you boys had gotten into other and more serious trouble. You should not take the guns out without either myself or the guide being with you."

"He was with us," interrupted Chunky.

"Then that was all right."

"But we didn't know he was with us, Professor," Tad Butler hastened to explain. "So we were in the wrong, even if he was along. However, it has turned out all right, and we've bagged two coyotes.

Wish we could take their pictures. Why didn't we think to bring a camera with us?"

"I think I can supply that," laughed the guide. "I always carry one with me. In the morning I'll take your pictures. I got a new camera in Eureka yesterday, having lost my old one in the blow-out we had the other night."

The boys gave three cheers and a tiger for Tom Parry.

# CHAPTER VII
## CHUNKY COMES TO GRIEF

Breakfast was cooked in the cool of the early dawn, long before the sun had pushed its burning course up above the desert sands. Though the boys had but little sleep, they tumbled out at the guide's first hail, full of joyous enthusiasm for what lay before them that day.

Stacy Brown emerged from his tent rubbing his eyes. The lads uttered a shout when they saw him.

"Look at him!" yelled Ned. "Look at Chunky's eye!"

The right eye was surrounded by a black ring, the eyelid being of the same dark shade, where the end of the telescope on his rifle had kicked him.

"Young man, you are a sight to behold," smiled the Professor.

"I don't care. I got the coyote," retorted Stacy, with a grin.

"And the gun got him," added Walter.

"Judging from your appearance, I should say that the butt of your rifle was almost as dangerous as the other end," laughed Tad.

"Come and get it!" called the guide.

The lads never had to be called twice for meals, and they were in their places at the breakfast table with a bound.

"Do you know, I'm beginning to like the sage brush taste in the food," said Walter.

Stacy made up a face.

"I should think you would be ashamed to sit down to a meal with that countenance of yours, Chunky," declared Ned.

"I might with some company."

"See here, Chunky Brown. Do you mean— —"

"I mean that my face will get over what ails it, but yours won't," was the fat boy's keen-edged retort.

"All of which goes to prove," announced Tad wisely, "that you never can tell, by the looks of a toad, how far it will jump. I guess you'd better let Chunky alone after this. He's perfectly able to take care of himself, Ned."

Ned subsided and devoted his further attention to his breakfast. The meal finished, all hands set briskly to work to strike camp. In half an hour the burros were loaded ready for the day's journey. The boys set off singing.

"I don't see how you can tell where you are going," said the Professor. "There is no sun and you have no compass."

"We are traveling almost due southwest. I never use a compass. It is not necessary."

"There, I knew I had forgotten to get something," announced Tad.

"Forgotten what?" questioned Walter.

"To get a compass."

"You have a watch, have you not?" asked Tom Parry.

"Why, yes; but that's not a compass."

"Oh, yes, it is," smiled the guide. "You can get your direction just as well with that as you could with a tested compass."

"Never heard that before," muttered Tad.

"Nor I," added Ned, at once keenly interested.

"I'm easy. I'll ask how? What's the answer?" questioned Stacy, gazing innocently at Tom Parry.

"I am not joking, boys. Every watch is a compass. You can get your direction from it unerringly whenever you can see the sun."

"Indeed?" marveled the Professor.

"The method is very simple," continued Parry. "All you have to do is to point the hour hand directly at the sun. Half way between the hour hand and the figure twelve on the watch dial you will find is due south."

"I'll try it," answered Tad.

"There comes the sun now," said Ned.

The boys drew out their watches, having halted the ponies and turned facing the rising sun.

"Well, did you ever!" exclaimed the lads in one voice.

"It is, indeed, the fact," marveled the Professor.

"You can depend upon that whenever you have lost your way," said Tom Parry. "It has helped me out on many occasions."

"But what if there isn't any sun—what if the sky is clouded?" questioned Stacy.

"Then you'll have to sit down and wait for it," laughed the guide.

After this brief rest the party continued on its way. They had come out on the level plain, and before them for several miles stretched the white alkali of the Nevada Desert. As the sun rose higher, they found the glare of the glistening plain extremely trying to the eyes. The guide suggested that they put on their goggles. But the boys would have none of them. Stacy's right eye was badly swollen, yet he refused to cover it, though the fine dust of the plain got into it, causing it to smart until the tears ran down his cheek.

"Where do the wild horses congregate?" asked Tad, riding up beside the guide.

"Likely to see them anywhere, though they do not, as a rule, go far out on the desert on account of the scarcity of water. We may see some in the Little Smoky Valley and the Hot Creek Range when we reach there."

"Is it difficult to catch them?"

"Very. There is one magnificent white stallion that the horse-hunters have been trying to capture for the past five years."

"Why can't they get him?"

"Too smart for them. He knows what they are up to almost as well as if the hunters had confided their plans to him. Twice, in the beginning, the hunters succeeded in getting him in a trap, but he managed to get away from his would-be captors."

"I'd like to get a chance to take him," mused Tad Butler.

"I'm afraid you wouldn't have much luck, but we'll have a hunt when we get down in the horse country, and I promise you that you will see some exciting sport. Better than hunting coyotes by moonlight," laughed the guide.

"I'd like to capture and break a real live wild horse," said young Butler, his eyes sparkling at the thought. "It would be a fine prize to take away with me, now wouldn't it?"

"If you chanced to capture a good one, yes. The poor stock, however, has been pretty well taken up, so that the horses on the ranges now are splendid specimens."

"Anybody want to run a race?" interrupted Stacy, riding up near the head of the procession.

"Too hot," answered Tad.

"Just the kind of a day for a horse race. I'll run any of you to see who cooks the supper," persisted Stacy.

"Oh, go back with the burros. I wouldn't eat any supper that you cooked, anyway."

"I'll remember that, Ned. Well, if none of you has spunk enough to race with me, I'll run a race with myself."

"That a dare?" questioned Walter.

Stacy nodded, blinking his blackened eye nervously.

Walter shook out the reins.

"Come on, then. I suppose you won't be satisfied until you've gotten into more trouble. Where do you want to race to?"

"See that patch of ground whiter than the rest off there?"

"Yes."

"Well, we'll race there and back. How far is it from here, Mr. Parry?"

"'Bout half a mile, I should say," answered the guide, measuring the distance with his eyes.

"Whew! I didn't think it was so far," marveled Stacy. "But we'll run it, anyway."

"I'll be the starter," announced Ned. "If you break your neck, Chunky, remember that I am not to blame for it."

"If I break my neck I won't be likely to remember anything, so you're safe," retorted Stacy.

The others were too busy discussing wild-horse hunting to give heed to the boys' plan.

"All ready!"

"Yes."

"Go!"

Both lads uttered a sharp yell, at the same time giving their spurs a gentle pressure, and away they went across the blazing alkali, their tough little ponies steaming in the intense heat as they straightened out, entering into the spirit of the contest with evident enthusiasm.

"See those boys ride," laughed the guide, pausing in his argument on the wild-horse question: "I didn't suppose the fat boy could sit in a saddle like that."

"Oh, yes; he does well. You saw him master the bucker the other day in the mountains?"

"Yes, I remember. Whoa! Look out, there! There goes one of them! He took too short a turn."

"Walter's down!" cried Ned.

"Hope he isn't hurt."

"No; he's cleared all right. That was a mighty quick move the way he slipped out of that saddle. It would have broken his leg sure, if the pony had fallen on it," declared the guide.

Stacy had pulled up his own mount after making the turn safely. Then he rode slowly back.

"Hurt you any, Walt?" he asked.

"Jarred me a little, that's all. Why don't you go on and win the race?"

"Waiting for you," announced the fat boy laconically.

Walter swung into his saddle.

"Come on, then. Gid-ap!" he cried, shaking out the reins.

The two little animals sprang away like projectiles. But Stacy seemed not to be in his best form. He came in bobbing up and down, several lengths behind Walter.

"You won the race. I fell off," announced Walter, with his usual spirit of fairness.

"I guess not," drawled Stacy. "Now I'm going to do some stunts."

With that, the fat boy galloped out over the alkali again, riding off fully half a mile ahead of the party, where he jogged back and forth for a time, then began riding in a circle.

After a little they saw him toss his hat into the air ahead of him, and putting spurs to his pony dart under it, giving it a swift blow with his quirt, sending it spinning some distance away, at the same time uttering a shrill whoop.

"Thinks he's having the time of his life," grunted Ned.

"For a boy with a black eye, he is particularly cheerful, I should say," laughed Parry. "What's he going to do now!"

"Pick up his sombrero while at a gallop, I guess," replied Tad, shading his eyes and gazing off across the plain. "Yes, there he goes at it."

Stacy, with a graceful dip from his saddle, swooped down on the sombrero, scooping it up with a yell of triumph, then dashing madly across the desert to the westward.

All at once they saw his pony stumble.

"There he goes!" warned the guide. "He will break his neck!"

Down plunged the broncho, his nose scraping the ground, his hind feet beating the air wildly.

Stacy kept right on.

"The pony struck a thin crust on the alkali," explained the guide.

Almost before the words were out of his mouth Stacy Brown hit the desert broadside on. Then, to the amazed watchers, he seemed to disappear before their very eyes.

"He's gone! What does it mean?" cried the boys.

Where but a few seconds before had been a pony and a boy, there now remained only a kicking, floundering broncho.

Tom Parry put spurs to his mount and set off at top speed for the scene of the accident, followed by the others of the party strung out in single file.

# CHAPTER VIII
# NEARLY DROWNED IN AN ALKALI SINK

Tad rapidly drew up on the guide.

"What has happened?" Butler cried as the two now raced along side by side.

"As I said before, the pony went through a thin crust— —"

"Yes, but Chunky—what happened to him?" asked Tad.

"He went through when he struck the ground."

"I don't understand it at all."

"You will when you get there."

Tad was mystified. The solution of the mystery was beyond him.

"If he isn't drowned, he's in luck," snapped Parry.

"Drowned?" wondered his companion.

They cleared the intervening space that lay between them and the fat boy's pony in a series of convulsive leaps that the bronchos took under the urgent pressure of the rowels of their riders' spurs.

As they neared the scene Tad espied a hole in the desert, and began to understand. Stacy also had struck a thin crust and had broken through. Yet what had happened to him after that, Tad did not know.

Both would-be rescuers leaped from their ponies and ran to the spot.

With his body submerged, his head barely protruding above the water, sat Stacy, vigorously rubbing his eyes to get the brown alkali water out of them sufficiently to enable him to look about and determine what had happened to him.

The rest of the party dashed up with loud shouts of alarm, hurling a series of rapid-fire questions at the guide.

Parry and Tad grasped Stacy by the arms and hauled him, dripping, from the alkali sink into which he had plunged.

They shouted with laughter when they saw that he was not hurt seriously.

"Well, of all the blundering idiots — —" began Ned.

"That will do," warned the Professor, hurrying to Stacy's side. "Hurt you much, lad?"

"I — I fell in," stammered Chunky.

"I should say you did. How in the world did it happen?"

The guide explained, that frequently these thin crusts were found on the desert, covering alkali sinks, some being dry, others having water in them.

"And of course Chunky had to find one. He's the original hoodoo," laughed Ned.

"Oh, I don't know," replied the guide. "He has done us a real service by falling in."

"How's that!" questioned Tad.

"Master Stacy has found a water hole, just what we need at this particular moment. The stock needs water, and especially the ponies that have been racing for the last half hour."

"You don't mean that we are to drink that stuff, do you?" demanded Walter.

"Not now. We still have some fairly good water in the water bags. Later on you may be glad to drink alkali water. Run up and down if you feel able. You'll dry off in a few minutes," suggested Parry, turning to Chunky.

"I — I don't want to. Feels nice and cool after my bath. Jump in and take a swim, fellows."

"No, thank you — not in that dirty water," objected Ned.

"I'll tell you what, boys," suggested Tad. "After the stock has had a drink we'll take off our shoes and put our feet in. Guess we can stand that much."

"That's a good idea," agreed Walter. "We'll all take a cold foot bath."

In the meantime, the guide had been busily engaged in breaking the crust around the sink, so that the stock might more easily get at the water within it. The animals were impatiently pawing and whinnying, anxious to get the water. They were now willing to drink any kind of water after their half day's journey across the burning alkali.

"You might unpack and get a cold lunch together, if you will," suggested Parry.

The boys soon had one of the tents erected, over which they stretched the fly, that the interior might be cooler.

Ned opened a can of pickled pigs' feet, which, with some hard rolls were spread out on a folding table under the tent. Tad, not to be out-done, dug some lemons from his saddle bag, with which he proceeded to make a pail of lemonade.

It was the first time they had had any such beverage since they began their summer trips. Tad had purchased the lemons back in Eureka. The lemonade made, it lacked only sweetening now.

"Where's the sugar?" he called.

"Where's the sugar?" echoed Chunky.

"We don't know," answered Ned and Walter in the same breath.

"Get busy and find it, then. If you don't want this lemonade I'll drink it myself. I don't care whether it is sweetened or not."

That threat was effective. The other three boys made a dive for the burros. An examination of the first pack failed to reveal the sweetening. The same was the case with the next, and before they had finished, their entire outfit was spread over the ground, tents, canned goods, cooking utensils, thrown helter-skelter over several rods of ground.

"Here, boys, boys!" chided the Professor. "This will never do. We can't afford to use our provisions in that way. Soon we'll have nothing."

"Regular rough house. Ought to be ashamed of yourselves," agreed Stacy, surveying the scattered outfit, while he secretly slipped two lumps of sugar into his mouth. "Here, cook, pick up your kitchen," to Ned.

"What you got in your mouth?" demanded Ned suspiciously.

"He's eating the sugar," spoke up Walter Perkins.

"Drop 'em!" roared Ned.

Stacy started to run, whereupon the boys fell upon him, and the next second he was at the bottom of the heap. The boys were rubbing his face in the sand in an effort to make him give up the sugar.

The Professor took a hand — two hands in fact — about this time. He made short work of the "goose pile," tossing the boys from the very much ruffled Stacy, whom he also jerked to his feet.

"What's all this disturbance about?" demanded Professor Zepplin. "First you strew the outfit all over the desert, then you get to pummeling each other."

"Chunky's been stealing sugar," volunteered Ned.

"Give back that sugar, instantly!" commanded the Professor.

The fat boy shook his head and grinned.

"Can't," he answered.

"And, why not?"

"'Cause they're inside of me."

"Now, now, now!" warned Ned. "You haven't chewed that hard sugar down this quick. I know better than that."

"No, I swallowed the lumps whole when you fellows jumped on me. Nearly choked me to death, 'cause one of 'em got stuck in my throat," Chunky explained.

Tad, in the meantime, had been busy gathering up the scattered provisions.

"Get to work, young gentlemen. Straighten up the camp," commanded the Professor.

"Don't we get any lunch?" begged Stacy.

"You're full of sugar. You don't need anything else," replied Walter.

"When you have set the outfit to rights, we'll all sit down and eat like civilized beings," asserted the Professor, with emphasis.

"Civilized beings making a meal on pigs' feet! Huh!" grumbled Chunky, picking up a can of tomatoes, then throwing it down again. After this, he slipped around to the opposite side of the tent. Crawling in under the fly he promptly went to sleep, the others being so busy that they had not observed his act.

The next Stacy knew was when he awakened to find himself being hauled out by one leg.

"Here, what are you doing? Leggo my foot."

"Lunch is ready. You ought to thank us, instead of finding fault because we woke you up. You might have slept right through the meal; then you wouldn't have had anything to eat," explained Walter.

Stacy shook his head.

"No danger. I wasn't afraid of that!"

"Not afraid of that? Why not?" demanded Ned.

"'Cause I knew you'd haul me out. Left my feet sticking out so you would."

Everybody roared. There was no resisting Stacy Brown's droll humor.

"Hopeless," averred the Professor, shrugging his shoulders.

"He's a wise one," differed the guide.

"Another name for laziness," nodded Ned.

"What's that disease they have down south?" asked Walter. "I heard the Professor and the postmaster talking about it back in Eureka."

"You mean the—the hook-worm disease?" grinned the guide.

"That's it. That's what Chunky's got. When a fellow is too lazy to do anything but eat, they say he's got the—the— —"

"The hook— —" finished the guide.

"That's what he ought to get," agreed Ned.

"Gentlemen, gentlemen!" corrected the Professor. "This is not a seemly topic for table discussion."

"But we eat pigs' feet," suggested Stacy in wide-eyed innocence.

The meal finished, amid laughter and jest, the party stowed their belongings, and after a brief rest, pushed on, having decided that they would feel the heat less in the saddle.

At sundown the travelers were still some distance from the water hole for which the guide was making.

"We'll have to go on," he said. "We may have to ride some time after dark."

"Will that be advisable?" questioned the Professor.

"Not advisable, but necessary. The stock must have their water you know."

So the party pushed on. The moon came up late in the evening, and the guide looking about him, discovered that they had borne too far to the east, which necessitated their covering some four miles more of alkali than would have been the case had they kept more closely to their course.

"It can't be helped," he laughed good-naturedly. "I guess the pigs' feet will last you until we make camp."

"How long will that be, Mr. Parry?" questioned Chunky anxiously.

"All of an hour and a half."

Stacy humorously took up his belt three holes.

"Got two more holes left to take in," he decided after examining the belt critically.

"That's a new way to measure distance and time, isn't it!" laughed the guide.

"How?" wondered Stacy.

"By the holes in your belt."

At eleven o'clock that night Tom Parry announced that they had arrived at the end of their day's journey.

"Where's the water? I don't see any water?" said Walter.

"After supper we'll look for it. I presume want something to eat first, don't you?" questioned the guide.

"Yes," shouted the lads in chorus. "We're nearly starved."

Bacon and coffee constituted the bill of fare for their late meal, which they ate out in the bright moonlight with the crackling camp-fire near by.

"This is fine," announced Tad, with which sentiment all the boys agreed. "Wish we could do this every night."

"Your supper would be breakfast after a few days," replied Parry.

"How's that!" questioned Ned.

"If you waited for moonlight, I mean. The moon comes up later every night, you know."

"That's so."

"We'd get hungry, wouldn't we?" chuckled Stacy.

"You wouldn't get. You always are," retorted Ned.

"Now, I'll show you how I know there is a water hole near here," said Parry after they had finished their late meal. "When I locate it, you boys may help me take the stock to it."

They walked back some twenty rods from where they had pitched the camp, Parry meanwhile hunting about as if in search of something that he had dropped.

"Nope. No water here," decided Stacy.

"You don't know. Ah! Here is what I am looking for."

The guide pointed to a heap of stones that rose some twelve inches above the ground. On the west side of the heap several stones had been placed in a row, thus forming an arm that extended or pointed almost due west.

"Know what that is?" asked Parry.

The lads shook their heads.

"That's a water marker. When a traveler across the desert finds a sink he indicates it either by a heap of stones, which he sticks in the ground, or by any other means at his command. For instance, this pile of stones tells me there is a water hole somewhere near by, and the arm points the way to it."

"Where is it, then?" wondered Walter. "I don't see any signs of water."

"Nor do I. We'll follow the direction indicated by the arm and see if we don't come up with a water tank somewhere close by," replied Parry.

With the guide leading the way, the others following in single file, they trailed away to the westward until, finally, they came to a slight depression in the ground.

"It should be near here," the guide informed them. "There it is. See that dark hole?"

The boys bounded forward, dropping on their knees by the opening into which they peered inquiringly.

Suddenly they uttered a yell, and, springing up, ran back as fast as their legs would carry them. As they did so, some dark object bounded from the water tank and leaped away into the sage brush.

"Goodness me, what was that?" cried Walter, after the boys had pulled up and faced about.

"Come back, come back. That was only a badger," laughed the guide.

"In the water?" asked Tad, who had stood his ground.

"No; so much the worse for us! There is no water there. No need to look. The tank is empty. Some wandering prospector has emptied it to save his burros and fill his canteen," announced the guide.

"What are we going to do, then!" queried Ned.

"Do without it. We shall have to give the stock a very little of our fresh supply, saving only enough out of it for our own breakfast and a canteen full apiece to take with us on the morrow. I think I shall be able to find a river about ten miles below here, providing it has not changed its course or gone dry. The water here in this country is as fickle as the desert itself."

"What if we should fail to find any?" breathed Tad.

"Well, you know, neither man nor beast can travel far on the desert without it. But we'll find some to-morrow. Don't worry," soothed the guide, though in his innermost heart he was troubled. That this water hole should prove to be dry did not promise well for those that were to follow.

# CHAPTER IX
# THE BOYS DISCOVER A RIVER

"Where's that river you were talking about?" demanded the lads when the outfit pulled up at noon next day.

"Don't you see it?" smiled Parry.

"Not a river," answered Ned, gazing about him, then allowing his glance to rest on the face of the guide to determine if Parry were making sport of them.

"I am not sure myself. I know where it should be. Whether it's there or not is another matter. Fetch the shovels and we'll soon find out."

"Finding a river with shovels!" muttered Stacy. "Huh! Who ever heard of such a thing?"

But as soon as the boys had returned with the digging implements, Parry swung the tools over his shoulder and strode confidently to the left of where they were encamped for the noonday rest.

The boys followed him full of curiosity.

Finally the guide threw down the tools and began to run his hands over the hot, yellow soil.

"Guess the sun's gone to his head," muttered Ned, as he squatted down to observe more closely what the guide was doing. The other three lads followed his example. In a moment they were on all fours, hopping about like so many quadrupeds.

Parry was shaking with laughter as he observed them.

"Bow! Bow wow!" barked Chunky, jumping on hands and feet, snapping his teeth together suggestively.

The boys looked at each other and burst out laughing. They had discovered all at once what a ridiculous figure they were making.

"Sun gone to your head, too, Chunky?" chuckled Ned. "Oh, no, I forgot; it's dog days," he added maliciously.

"Your master had better get a collar and chain for you, then, Ned," laughed Stacy, in high good humor with himself.

The guide's voice put a sudden end to their merriment.

"Here's the river," he cried. "There is plenty of water in it, too."

The boys gathered about him quickly.

"I don't see any river," averred Walter.

"There isn't any," answered Ned, in a low voice.

"I'll show you whether there is or not," snapped Parry, who had overheard the remark. "You boys think I have gone crazy, don't you? You'll find there is something to learn about this old Nevada Desert—some things that you never even dreamed of. Hand me a shovel, please."

All at once Stacy began pushing his companions roughly aside.

"Here, here, Fatty! What are you trying to do?" the others demanded, beginning to struggle with him to prevent being bowled over.

"I'm saving your lives," cried the fat boy.

"Saving our lives?" cried Ned. "Go shake the alkali out of your eyes."

"Yes, you'll fall in and drown."

"In what?"

"In the river. Don't you see the river right there in front of you?" queried Stacy, his eyes fairly beaming with importance.

"No, I don't. If there was a river there you'd be the first one to fall in, and don't you forget that."

"What's this? What's this?" inquired the Professor, approaching.

"It's a river," answered Stacy solemnly.

"A river?"

"Yes, sir. Don't you hear it roar? Wish I had a boat."

"Is it water you are digging for, Mr. Parry?" asked Professor Zepplin.

But the guide did not hear the question. He was too busy with his mining operations at the moment.

"Come on, boys," he urged. "Get busy here."

"At what?" asked Ned. "We're with you, but we don't know what you want us to do."

"Yes; can we help you?" inquired Tad.

"Of course you can. Get those other shovels and dig."

"Where?"

"Right here. Make the dirt fly as fast as you want to. I'll show you something in a minute."

He did. All at once the sand beneath them gave way, and the Pony Rider Boys, all except Stacy Brown, uttered a yell as they sank waist deep into a sink of soft, wet sand.

Parry had felt the sand giving way, and with a warning had leaped from the hole. The lads had not been quick enough.

"There's no danger. Don't be alarmed. You'll get wet feet, that's all."

"What is it?" asked the Professor in amazement.

"Water, my dear sir. Water in plenty. It's a branch of the Pancake River. These streams run underground for great distances on the desert, but they change their course so often that you can't place any dependence on them. We're lucky, boys."

"Hurrah for the water!" shouted the lads.

"Keep on digging. We haven't got it yet. Master Stacy, will you run to the camp and bring the folding buckets? We'll soon have the hole cleaned so we can dip up some water."

"Sure," answered the fat boy, thrusting his hands in his trousers pockets and strolling off at a leisurely gait as if there were no necessity for haste.

"That's Chunky's idea of running," laughed Ned Rector, jerking his head in Stacy's direction.

The three lads finding there was no danger in their position, had made no attempt to clamber from the hole. Instead, they began digging, until the dirt flew so fast that the Professor was obliged to withdraw. Somehow most of the dirt seemed to be flying through the air right in his direction.

Now the water began to rise above the caved-in sand. It was a dirty yellow in color and the boys' clothing suffered as a result. But the youngsters did not care. Besides, they were cooling off.

At last the hole had been cleared sufficiently to enable them to dip up some water, but Stacy not having returned with the pails, the Professor was sent to fetch him. He found the lad enjoying himself tickling the nose of a drowsy burro.

Professor Zepplin led Chunky out to the water sink, by one ear. The lads now quickly dipped up pailful after pailful, which they passed to the guide on the bank. He ran with them to the stock, giving each of the animals a little, so that all might share in the first instalment. Ponies and burros were wide awake now, expressing their pleasure in loud whinnies and blatant brays.

"It's foggy on the river," laughed Ned. "The burros have started up their fog horns."

When Parry returned he brought with him the drinking cups, which he had taken from the saddles.

"Is it fit to drink?" asked Tad as the cups were passed down to them.

"It's wet."

"So are we," retorted Ned. "But we're dirty. Uh! That's horrible stuff."

"Strongly alkaline," nodded the Professor, after sipping gingerly at the brimming cup Parry had passed to him. "Do you not think we had better wait a little while until it settles?"

"Not a second, if you're thirsty," answered the guide shortly. "This stream is liable to change its course in the next ten minutes. Don't you take any chances with a desert stream. Fill the water bags and the canteens as fast as we can that's what we'll do. Then, if the water holds out, there will be time enough to empty out our supply and fill with fresh."

"Hey, Chunky! Haul those water bags over here," called Walter.

"Can't," called Stacy. He was sitting on the ground pulling off a shoe.

"What's the trouble now?" snorted Ned. "Got a cramp?"

"No; I've got a sore toe."

"Supposing we duck him," suggested Ned.

"We'll save all the water we have," warned the guide sharply. "No nonsense about it, either."

The party was in great good humor, now that they had found a water hole, and the animals had drunk until their sides were distended like balloons in process of being inflated.

"They've had enough," announced the guide, going to the animals and glancing over the herd sharply. "No more water for the present."

"Then perhaps we might as well be on our way," suggested the Professor.

Parry did not reply. He was shading his eyes with one hand, gazing intently off over the desert. The Professor, following the direction in which the guide was looking, discovered a cloud of dust rising into the air. The cloud was approaching them at a rapid rate.

# CHAPTER X
## A COWBOY TAKES A HEADER

"What is that?" questioned Professor Zepplin sharply.

"That's what I'm trying to make out," replied the guide.

"Looks like horsemen."

"Yes, it is. But I can't understand why they can be riding at that killing pace on a hot afternoon such as this."

About this time the boys' attention had been attracted to the yellow cloud by Stacy Brown, who, notwithstanding his apparent slowness, had sharp eyes when there was anything to be seen.

"Somebody's coming," he announced between sips.

"What's that?" demanded Tad, springing from the water hole, followed closely by Walter and Ned.

"Somebody coming to pay us an afternoon call. By the way they're whooping it up they must be in a hurry about something."

All hands ran to where Mr. Parry and the Professor were standing.

The yellow cloud was rolling toward them at a rapid pace, and ahead of it the boys discovered half a dozen horsemen, who had evidently discovered the white tent that the Pony Rider Boys had erected during their midday stop.

"Know them?" asked Tad.

"I'm not sure, but I think it's Bud Stevens and the wild-horse outfit. Judging from the way they ride they're pretty wild themselves."

With a series of shrill "y-e-o-w-s," the strangers bore down on the little desert camp. From the gray, alkali-flecked backs of the ponies clouds of steam were rising, their sides streaked with dust and sweat.

"Whoop! Hooray!" bellowed the newcomers, dashing up to the camp, letting go a volley of revolver shots right into the ground in front of the Pony Rider Boys.

Not a boy flinched.

"How!" said Tom Parry.

"How!" roared Bud Stevens, the leader, throwing himself from the back of his trembling mount.

"Where's the boss?" asked Parry.

"He's gone down Ralston way."

"Thought so. Where you headed?"

"San Antone Range after more hoss flesh. We'll rope the white stallion this time, and don't you forget it. Eh, kiddie? You're the little coyote what roped my pony and plunked me into the street back in Eureka, ain't you?"

Half jokingly, he swung a vicious blow at Tad with the flat of his hand. Had it landed it would have laid the lad flat.

Tad ducked and came up smiling.

"Wow! The kiddie's a regular little bantam. We'll have to take a fall out of you. Got to give you the desert initiation like they do in the secret societies back in Eureka."

He sought to close with Tad, but the boy eluded him easily.

"That'll do, Bud," warned the guide, stepping between them. "No rough house here. Want some water? We've got a water hole right over there."

"Water? Water? Call the stuff we get out of the ground here water?"

"He—he's had his head in soak already," piped Stacy, noting the perspiration dripping from the cowboy leader's face.

Parry gave the lad a warning look.

"They're good enough fellows, but they are full of pranks when they are not at work. No need to stir them up and make them mad."

"Got anything to eat?" demanded Bud.

"How would you like some coffee, sir?" asked Tad politely.

"Coffee?" jeered the cowboy. "Now what d'ye think of that, fellows? Ain't that right hospitable?"

"Yes, thank you, young man, I guess that would touch the spot," spoke up another of the band. "'Course we'll have some coffee."

"All right. Ned, will you and Walt fix something for the boys to eat? If you will lead your ponies over to the water hole I'll dip up some water for them in the meantime, gentlemen."

"Kiddie, yer all right," bellowed Bud Stevens. "But I've got to take a fall out of yer yet."

"Some other time," grinned Tad, who felt no fear of the hulking cowboy.

"See that nose?" demanded Bud, sticking out his head at Tad.

"Yes; what's the matter?"

"That's my nose. And that's where I barked it when you roped my pony tother day. Oh, I've got to take it out of yer hide, kiddie."

"Come along. We'll water the ponies. Chunky, help lead those bronchos to the water hole, will you?"

The two boys and the noisy plainsmen gathered the tired animals and led them to the hole that had been dug in the desert. Stacy sprang in and began dipping out pails of water.

Bud grabbed the first pailful, but instead of offering it to one of the thirsty animals, he deliberately emptied the contents over the head of the boy down in the hole.

"Hi, there! Stop that, will you?" howled Stacy Brown.

The fat boy was mad all through.

He scrambled from the hole, dragging a slopping pail of water after him, while Bud Stevens roared with delight. But his mirth was short-lived.

Stacy ran around the hole and straight at the cowboy who had soaked him with the yellow water. Up went the pail.

Splash!

The contents of it were hurled full in the face of the wild cowboy, who at that moment, having his mouth wide open, got a mouthful of it.

The battle was on instantly. Tad knew it was coming, but he did not think it would be directed at him this time, though he realized that he would have to protect his companion at any cost.

Choking and sputtering, Bud made a blind lunge at Tad, his eyes being so full of muddy water that he could barely make out the slender form of the Pony Rider Boy.

Tad ducked and dodged, hoping that Stevens would tire of pursuing him in a moment. The lad might have called to the others over by the camp, but he was too proud to do that. He would fight his own battles, no matter what the odds were against him.

"I've got to get in," muttered the lad. "He's seeing clearer every minute, and the longer I wait the less chance I'll have of getting out with a whole skin.

"I'm coming, kiddie!" roared Bud.

Tad made no reply.

Stooping as if for a spring, Butler launched himself straight at the pillar of brawn and muscle before him. Had he hesitated for the briefest part of a second—had he permitted those muscular arms to close about him, Tad Butler would have gone down to a quick and inglorious defeat.

But he did not wait.

The lad's right arm was brought sharply against the neck of his adversary, while at the same time his left arm was slipped under the cowboy's right leg. The result was that Stevens lurched to the left. A quick jerk and Bud was fairly lifted from the ground.

Tad gave a quick, forceful tug.

Bud Stevens landed on his head in the pool of yellow water, his feet beating the air wildly.

**Bud Stevens Landed on His Head in the Pool of Yellow Water**

"Grab hold of a foot, Chunky!" commanded Tad. "Quick! He'll drown in a minute in there."

"Oh, let 'im drown," drawled Stacy, blinking to get the sand out of his eyes.

"Get hold, I tell you! I'll thrash you, Stacy Brown, if you don't!"

Stacy reluctantly complied, Tad in the meantime having grasped the cowboy's foot and began pulling.

"Not that way, Chunky. Do you want to pull him apart?"

The fat boy was trying to get Bud's right leg out from the opposite side of the water hole.

The disturbance had by this time attracted the attention of the men over in the camp. They started on the run when they saw Bud turned head first into the water hole.

By the time they reached the scene Tad and Stacy had succeeded in hauling the victim from his perilous position. Bud was choking between roars of rage. His companions went off into shrieks of laughter when they understood what had happened. They rolled on the ground; they danced about their fallen companion, and then their revolvers began to add their vicious voices to the tumult.

Tad paid no attention to the uproar. He was too busy shaking the water out of his fallen antagonist, to whom he was giving first aid to the drowning.

Bud staggered to his feet, gasped for breath, while Tad stepped off a few paces, so as not to be within reach of those long, bony arms, should Bud decide to stretch them forth and take him in.

"Guess you got all that was coming to you that time, Bud Stevens," grinned Tom Parry. "Served you right. You'll let those boys alone after this or you'll have to reckon with me."

Stevens's face was streaked with wet sand, his hair was disheveled and his clothes stuck to him as if they had been pasted on.

The cowboy's sullen face slowly relaxed into a mirthless grin.

"Say, kiddie, you put it over me like a cactus plant. I owe you two."

"I'd cancel the debt if I were in your place," laughed the boy. "Come along and have a drink of coffee. It'll warm you up after your swim."

# CHAPTER XI
# A PIECE OF HUMAN SANDPAPER

An appetizing meal had been spread for the visitors. But every time the men glanced at their companion they broke out into loud guffaws.

"You're a sight, Bud," jeered one.

"Next time better take a man of your size," said another.

"Guess that's right," grinned the vanquished one. "Ye can't most always tell what a kid's going to do."

"We know what this one did do to you, though," laughed another.

"Reckon I do myself," admitted Stevens. "Say, kiddie, you come along with us and try them tricks on the wild hosses we're going to catch. Mebby I'll forgit to take it out of you. I'll let the white stallion do that."

"Thank you; I'll accept that invitation, with Professor Zepplin's permission."

"We intended to drop in on your bunch, anyway," interposed Parry. "The boss has invited us to join a horse hunt with you."

"Better go along with us now, then," suggested Stevens. "We won't have no more rough house, leastwise till we get to the San Antone Range, eh?"

"No," replied Parry. "We have a pack train to drag along. Besides, you fellows travel too fast for us. We'll take our time and join you later."

The bath and the hot coffee had served to quiet Bud Stevens's bubbling spirits. He was by this time a more rational being.

After they had finished the meal Bud drew Tad Butler aside confidentially.

"Say, kiddie, I like you," he said, slapping the lad a violent blow between the shoulders.

"Glad of it," laughed Tad. "But you have a queer way of showing your affection."

"Say, can you ride?"

"Some," admitted Tad.

"As well as you can fight and throw a rope?"

"I was not aware that I did either one very well."

"Go away! Go away! You're a champeen. I've got a spavined, ring-boned cayuse over in the range that I'm going to put you up against when you join us. He'll give you all the exercise you want——"

"Hey, Bud, ain't it 'bout time we were moseying?" called one of Stevens's companions.

"I reckon. Can't be any hotter than 'tis now. When you going to join us, Parry?"

"We'll be there in a few days. But come here; I want to talk with you?"

"Sure thing."

"If we go on a hunt with you, remember there's to be no funny business. These boys, while they're no tenderfeet, are fine fellows and they must be treated well. I'm responsible for them. What I say goes. Understand?"

"We'll look out for the kids, don't you get in a hot stew 'bout that."

With a final whoop and a cheer for the members of Tom Parry's party, the turbulent cowboys put spurs to their ponies. Once more a cloud of dust rose from the desert, across which it slowly rolled. The boys watched it for half an hour, until the cloud had dwindled to a mere speck in the distance.

"Not such a bad lot, after all," was the Professor's conclusion.

"Rough diamonds," smiled the guide.

"Are we going on now, Mr. Parry?" asked Tad.

"No; I think we may as well unpack and make camp here until to-morrow morning. Then the stock will be fresh, and so shall we."

"The stock looks to be in pretty good shape already," answered Tad.

"Yes; but they will be much better to-morrow. A day's water and feed will do wonders for them. I guess the bunch of horse-hunters made quite a hole in our fodder, didn't they?"

"There was nothing the matter with their appetites that I observed," laughed Tad. "But we've got enough to last us for some time. How long before we shall strike the range where we are to join them?"

Parry glanced off over the desert meditatively.

"If we have no bad luck we ought to make it in three days. The cowboys will get there some time to-morrow."

"One of them won't," answered Tad, confidently.

"Why not?"

"His pony is wind-broken. Didn't you hear him breathe when they rode in?"

"What, with the bunch howling like a pack of coyotes? No, I didn't hear a horse breathe."

"I did," chimed in Stacy.

"Did what?" queried Ned, turning on him sharply. Rector had not heard the fat boy approach them.

"Heard the big cowboy breathe. He wheezed like a leaky steam engine."

Tad and the guide burst out laughing.

"Why, boy, we weren't talking about the cowboy. We were speaking of one of the bronchos. Tad says he is wind-broken."

"Huh!" grunted Stacy, strolling off with hands thrust in his pockets, chin on his breast. "When I'm not right I'm always wrong," he muttered. "Mostly wrong."

They did not see the lad again for more than an hour. The rest of the party gathered under the tent they had first erected, where they now fell to discussing their late visitors, next turning to their plans for the morrow.

"Do we follow the same course when we next start?" asked the Professor.

"Not quite. We veer a little more to the west, until we string the San Antonio Range. When we leave there, if you conclude to go on, we shall head southward toward Death Valley. I understand you are willing to penetrate it a little way."

"Yes, if you think it is safe to do so."

Parry shrugged his shoulders.

"Death Valley is no better than its name. If you wish merely to see it, I think I can gratify your desire."

"Yes, yes, we want to see Death Valley," chorused the boys. "Don't be afraid for us."

"I'll try to get some water bags from the horse-hunters when we join them; for the further south one goes on the desert the more scarce the water becomes."

The sun was lying low by this time and the advance guard of the evening coolness began crowding back the heat of the day.

"I wonder what has become of Chunky?" questioned Tad suddenly, rising from the ground where he had thrown himself in the shade of the tent.

The others glanced quickly about them.

"Probably find him asleep behind a bunch of sage somewhere," answered Ned lightly. "Don't trouble yourself about him."

"Perhaps over by the water hole," suggested the guide. "I'll stroll over that way."

Just then a figure topped the ridge beyond them.

It was yelling lustily, leaping into the air, rolling and groveling on the ground alternately.

"There he is! Something's happened to him," shouted Walter.

All hands started on a run. They could not imagine what had gone wrong with the fat boy.

As they drew nearer to him they discovered that he had taken off all his clothes. His body was as red as if it had been painted.

The Professor's long legs were covering the alkali at a pace that left the others behind, until Tad spurted and headed him.

"Chunky, Chunky! What's the matter?" he shouted.

Stacy yelled more lustily than ever.

"What is it? What is it?" shouted the others in chorus.

"I'm burned alive? I'm cremated! Oh, w-o-w!"

"Should think you would he. What on earth have you got your clothes off for?"

They discovered that something was the matter then, for an expression of real pain had taken the place of the complacent look they were wont to see on the face of Stacy Brown.

"He's been boiling himself!" exclaimed the guide, with quick intuition.

Grasping the fat boy, Parry threw him flat on the ground and began rolling him in the sand. Stacy yelled more lustily than before.

"Run to my saddlebags. Fetch the black bottle you will find there!" commanded the guide. "It's oil, yes. Hurry, before his skin all peels off."

Tad was back with the black bottle in no time. Tom Parry spread the oil over the blistered flesh of the fat boy, whose yells grew less and less explosive as he felt the soothing effects of the grease on his body.

"Wha—what happened?" stammered Walter.

"I—I fell in."

"In where?" questioned the Professor sharply.

"I don't know. It was hot."

"Put your clothes on. You'll be all right in a little while. Where did you leave them?"

Stacy pointed back on the desert some distance, whereat Parry laughingly said he would go in search of the clothing.

"Now if you will be good enough to tell me what all this uproar is about, I shall be obliged to you," requested the Professor.

"Why, the boy found a boiling spring——"

"And he fell in," added Ned solemnly.

"He did," agreed the guide, without the suspicion of a smile.

"Is that it, Master Stacy?"

Stacy nodded.

"Tell me about it."

"I—I was walking along with my hands in my pockets——"

"Thinking," interjected Ned.

"What'd you suppose I was doing! Ain't I always thinking when I'm not asleep?"

"Go on, go on," urged Ned unsympathetically.

"All at once something slipped. I went right through the ground. At first I thought I was a pond of ice water, it felt so cold. Next thing I knew I was burning up."

"But your clothes? What did you have them off for?" urged the Professor.

"I took them off when I thought I was burning up. Say, fellows, that was the hottest ice water I ever took a bath in my life."

The boys could barely resist their inclination to laugh.

"Why don't you laugh if you want to? Never mind me. I don't count," growled Chunky.

Parry explained that these boiling springs were not infrequent on the desert. They were found, generally, further north, he said. This one must have worked its way up through the alkali until only a thin crust covered it, and this crust the boy had had the misfortune to step on and break through.

"You wouldn't think there were so many pitfalls under this baked desert, would you?" questioned Ned.

"I look like a piece of human sandpaper, don't I?" muttered Stacy ruefully, as he carefully drew on his clothes. "Every time I sit down I'll remember that hot ice water."

# CHAPTER XII
## RUNNING DOWN THE TRAIL

"Thank goodness, we're in the foothills," sighed Tad, when three days later they came to a halt at the base of the San Antonio Range far down on the Nevada Desert.

"Yes, it is a relief to see some real rocks once more," agreed Walter. "Chunky, look out that you don't step into any more ice water. You'll miss the horse-hunt if you do."

"No danger of that up here," laughed the guide.

Behind them lay the desert maze, to the right and left, mountain ranges, high plateaux, mesas and buttes. Giant yucca trees, short, spreading piñon and spindling cedars clothed the higher peaks of the San Antonio Range.

Trees, too, were scattered about in the foothills, and though they gave little shade it was a relief to every sense of the Pony Riders to feel the hills and trees about them.

There, with what little shade they could get, the lads made camp. As yet they had found no water, though Parry said there would be springs in plenty further up in the mountains. The bags still held enough to last them until the following day, so no effort was made to locate fresh water that afternoon.

Stacy had thrown himself down under one of the yucca trees, but the late afternoon sun filtered through the branches, making his face look red and heated.

"You don't seem to be getting much shade from that tree," laughed the guide.

"'Bout as much as I would from a barbed wire fence," frowned Stacy.

"What do you know about barbed-wire fences?" demanded Ned.

"Me? Know all 'bout them. One night I had a falling out with one, when I was taking a short cut across the fields to get home."

"How about the apples? Did you get them?" asked Tad.

"Apples? What do you know 'bout it? Were you there, too?"

A laugh greeted the fat boy's reply.

"Come, come, young men. Are you going to make camp?" urged the Professor.

"Didn't know we were going to remain here to-night," replied Walter. "Of course we're going to make camp if that's the case. It'll be a good time to shake the alkali dust out of our belongings and from ourselves."

"I haven't got any dust," piped Stacy. "I—I had a bath—a hot bath."

"Are we anywhere near the horse-hunters, Mr. Parry?" inquired Tad, as the boys began unpacking the burros, some devoting their attention to the kitchen outfit, the rest spreading the canvas on the ground preparatory to erecting the tents.

"They are supposed to be further up the range. They will be down this way to-morrow, probably, to pick us up. They were not certain where they would make their permanent camp, Stevens said. All depends upon where the wild horses are grazing."

"I don't see any wild horses, nor any other wild anything," objected Ned.

The guide dropped the ridge pole that he was about to carry to the place where the cook tent had been laid out ready to be raised.

"Come with me," he said, taking Ned by the arm and leading him to the left of their camping place. "Do you see that?"

"What?"

"Use your eyes. If you're going to be a plainsman you'll have to depend on your sense of sight. Take the desert for instance. It's a desert maze if you are unable to read its signs; no maze at all if you do."

"What is it you were going to show Ned?" asked the rest of the boys, who had followed them out.

"See if you can tell, Master Tad."

But Master Tad had already been using his eyes. He nodded as he caught the guide's eye.

"There has been a bunch of unshod ponies along here, if that is what you mean," he said.

"How do you know?" demanded Stacy.

"I see their tracks there. Saw them the minute I got over here."

"Maybe that's the crowd that called at our camp the other day," suggested Walter.

The guide shook his head.

"There was no one on these horses," said Tad.

"Right," emphasized the guide. "That's observation, young men. You will notice, by examining these hoofprints carefully, that the weight of the animal is thrown more on the toe — —"

"How do you know that?" cut in Stacy.

"Because the toe sinks into the soil more than it would if the animals were loaded. In the latter event, the heels would dig deeper. Now if you will follow along a little further I may be able to show you the hoofprints of the leader of the band of wild horses, for that is what they are — —"

"Wild horses?" marveled the boys.

"Wish we could see them," said Tad.

"I'll wager they have seen us already, for they surely are in this neighborhood," replied Parry. "But a wild horse is as sharp as an old fox. The herd have been down in the foothills and, by the hoofprints, you will observe that they have returned to the mountain fastness."

"Perhaps they saw us coming," suggested Tad.

"More than likely," agreed the guide. "They were in a hurry and moving rapidly — there! There's the leader's trail. Look carefully and you will see where he leaped up to this little butte here. Reaching it, he turned about and took a quick, comprehensive look at the desert."

"And at us," added Stacy.

"Yes, I think so. Come up here. You see this little ridge gave him a very good view of the desert maze. See if you can tell how many wild horses there were in the bunch," suggested Tom Parry.

Instantly the boys went down on all fours, crawling along the trail seeking to read the story that it told.

"Well, how many?" queried the guide, after they had finished their inspection.

"Fifty!" shouted Stacy.

"Forty-five!" answered Ned and Walter at the same time.

"What do you say, Master Tad?"

"I am afraid I must have missed some, then. I only make out twenty-one old ones and a colt. I take it the old mare was with the colt, for the prints show that the little animal was hugging the other closely," was Tad's decision.

"Very good. Very good," nodded Parry. "There were twenty-two. You didn't get the trailer, probably an old mare. She traveled along off to the right yonder a little. But I should like to know how you made fifty, Master Stacy!" twinkled the guide.

"Counted 'em," answered the fat boy.

"Show me?"

Stacy did so, going over the hoofprints carefully, pointing to them with his index finger as he did so, the guide making mental calculations at the same time.

"And that makes fifty—fifty—fifty-four this time. There's more of them than I thought."

Parry laughed softly.

"I'm afraid you'd make a poor Indian, young man. You not only have counted the hoof-prints, but you have counted the foot marks of yourself and your companions as well. Master Tad, let me see if you can run the trail up the mountain side a little way. It will be good practice. I want you boys to be able to follow a trail as keenly as the best of them before you have finished this trip. You never know when it's going to be useful—when it's going to get you out of serious difficulties, even to the extent of saving your lives."

Tad was off on a trot, stooping well over, with eyes fixed on the foot marks.

"Tad could hunt jack rabbits without a dog, couldn't he?" questioned Stacy innocently. His companions laughed.

"Is that a joke?" asked Ned. "If it is, I'll cry. Your jokes would make a Texas steer weep."

Tad was picking his way up the rough mountain side, now losing the trail, then picking it up again. The marks left by the wild horses were almost indistinguishable after the animals had reached the rocks, but here and there a broken twig told the lad they had passed that way.

Once he appeared to leave the trail, moving sharply to the right, where on a shelving ridge, he straightened up and looked down into the valley.

Tom Parry nodded encouragingly.

"Know what you've found?"

"Yes, this is where the leader came to make another observation," answered Tad.

"That's right. He's a plainsman already, boys. Go on. Run the trail up to the top of this first ridge. It will not be a bad idea for us to know which way they've gone. If the hunters don't show up by to-morrow we can take a little run after the herd on our own hook."

Tad obeyed gladly. Every sense was on the alert. The rest of the boys were all impatience to take part in the hunt. But the guide said no. He feared that, if all were to start up the mountain side, their enthusiasm might lead them too far from camp, resulting in their losing their way. He knew how tricky the trail of a band of wild horses was, the clever animals leaving no ruse untried that would tend to mix up and lose their pursuers.

Tad's figure was growing smaller as he ascended higher and higher.

"You don't mean to say that horses climbed up the way he is going!" questioned Walter incredulously.

"That's the way they went, my boy. They're regular goats when it comes to mountain climbing. They'll go where a man could not, oftentimes."

Tad crept, cautiously on, now finding little to guide him, save his own instinct. He finally disappeared behind the rocks and trees of the low-lying range.

The lad was moving almost noiselessly now. A sound a short distance beyond him caused him to prick up his ears sharply.

"I believe I am near them," he breathed, as he glanced about him. "Why did I not think to bring my rope?"

It was just as well for his own well-being, that he had not brought along that part of his saddle equipment. He was following the trail with the skill of a trained mountaineer. An Indian himself could have done it no better.

Perhaps the guide understood, better than did Tad himself, why he had started the lad on the trail, for a quiet smile hung about the lips of Tom Parry. All at once his twinkling eyes lit up with a new expression.

"Look! Look!" gasped Walter.

"Where? Where?" demanded Ned.

Walter pointed to a pyramid-shaped rock far above their heads.

At first they could scarcely believe their senses. There poised in the air, feet doubled into a bunch, stood a splendid specimen of horseflesh, resting, it seemed, fairly on the sharp point of the rock, gazing down into and across the valley.

"The white stallion," breathed the lads all in the same breath.

The magnificent animal was a creamy white. Its head was held high, nostrils distended as if to catch the scent of those for whom it was looking. Beneath the rays of the low lying sun, its coat glistened and shone with a luster that no brush or comb could bring to it.

The lads gazed upon the beautiful statue almost in awe.

They were standing quite close up under the shadow of the mountain at that moment.

"Why doesn't he run?" whispered Walter.

"Do you think he sees us?" asked Ned.

"No. Stand perfectly still."

"Why doesn't he? All he would have to do would be to look down?" questioned Stacy.

"He scents us. He knows we are somewhere near. But, if you will observe him closely, you will notice that he is looking at the camp. He sees the Professor moving about," explained Parry.

"Do—do you think we could catch him?" asked Ned eagerly.

"The most skillful men in this part of the country have been trying to do that very thing for the last five years, my boy," answered the guide in a low tone. "No, you couldn't catch him. He's the finest animal to be found in the entire Nevada Desert district. Wouldn't mind owning him myself."

In the meantime Tad had been creeping nearer and nearer. He soon discovered that the leader of the band had swerved to the left. He concluded to follow, to see where the solitary animal had gone to. But so quietly did the lad move that the stallion neither heard nor scented him.

All at once the wonderful sight unfolded before the eyes of Tad Butler. He flattened himself on the ground, within thirty yards of the splendid animal.

Suddenly the stallion whirled. Tad rose to his feet, The two stood facing each other, Tad with head thrust forward, the stallion with nostrils held high in the air.

"Oh, my rope, my rope!" breathed the boy. "If I had my rope!"

# CHAPTER XIII
## COYOTES JOIN IN THE CHORUS

Those down in the foothills saw the animal whirl and face the other way.

"He sees something," cried Walter, forgetting in his excitement that they were trying to keep quiet.

"Yes, he has probably scented Master Tad," explained the guide.

"Think he'll try to catch the horse?" asked Stacy.

"Hope not. Those wild horses are bad medicine. No, of course, he has no rope with him. But he'll be wise if he keeps out of the way of the beast."

Tad had no thought of doing either. He stood perfectly still, gazing in awe and wonder at the handsomest horse he had ever seen.

The stallion's eyes blazed. He uttered a loud snort, then rose right up into the air on his hind feet. One bound brought him many feet nearer the boy who was observing him. It was the only direction in which the stallion could go without plunging into a chasm.

"Whoa!" commanded Tad sharply.

The white horse never having been trained, failed to understand the word, but he halted just the same, gazing angrily at the bold boy standing there, who, it appeared, was defying him.

Uttering another snort, this time full of menace, the animal leaped straight toward the lad in long, graceful bounds.

Tad threw up his hands to frighten the stallion aside. The animal, however, refused to be swerved from its course.

"He's going to run over me," cried the boy, as he noted that the horse was rising for another leap.

Tad ducked just as the beast sprang clear of the ground. He felt the rush of air as the gleaming body was lifted over his head, the boy at the instant uttering a shrill yell to hasten the stallion's movements.

The front hoofs caught the rim of the Pony Rider Boy's sombrero, snipping it from his head. The hind feet came closer. They raked Tad's head, bowling him completely over, rolling him from the knoll on which he had been standing.

He brought up with a jolt some ten feet further down. Tad scrambled to his feet a little dizzy from the blow and the fall.

"Whew! That was a close call," he muttered, feeling his head to learn if it had been injured.

"No; the skin isn't broken, but I'm going to have a beautiful goose egg there," he concluded. "It's swelling already. If I'd had my rope I could have roped him easily when he rose at me that last time."

Scrambling up the bank, Tad found his hat. Then he picked his way to the pyramid-shaped rock on which he had first discovered the stallion.

Poising himself, he swung his sombrero to his companions down in the foothills.

"Hurrah!" he shouted. "I met the enemy. I've seen the white stallion, fellows!"

"Is the enemy yours?" jeered Ned Rector.

"No; I rather think I was his," laughed Tad, turning back and hurrying down the rocks to rejoin his companions.

He was met by a volley of questions the moment he reached the foothills. With his companions gathered about him, Tad told them how he had followed the trail, finally coming upon the handsome animal while the latter was taking an observation from the pyramid-shaped rock.

"It's a wonder he didn't attack you," said the guide after the lad had finished his narration. "Those wild stallions are very savage when aroused."

"I guess he tried to do so all right," laughed Tad.

"I knew he was up there somewhere, watching us, but I did not think for a minute that you would get close enough to him to be in any danger," announced Tom Parry, with a disapproving shake of his head.

"I could have roped him easily," said the lad.

"Lucky for you that you didn't try it. It's getting late now. I presume the Professor is beginning to think we are not going to finish pitching our camp. Come, we'll go back and get to work."

The work went rather slowly, however, for the lads were too full of the subject of the wild stallion to devote their whole attention to putting their camp to rights for the night. Then again, they had to go all over the story for the Professor's benefit.

"Do you think we could catch one of these wild ones to take back East with us?" asked Tad.

"You couldn't catch one yourself, but you might be able to buy one for a small sum from the horse-hunters," the guide informed him.

"How much?"

"Depends on the animal. Perhaps twenty or twenty-five dollars."

"Then, I'll do it. I could get him home for as much more, and he'd be worth at least two hundred dollars. Perhaps I might take two of them along, providing I can get what I want."

"You ought to be a horseman," laughed the guide. "You've got the horseman's instinct."

"He is a horseman," volunteered Stacy. "There aren't any better."

"Thank you," glowed Tad. "I'll pull you out next time you fall in, for that."

They were very jolly at supper that night. They had nothing to trouble them. Water was near by and they were soon to participate in the most exciting event in their lives, a wild-horse hunt.

"Do you think they will be able to find us!" questioned Walter.

"Who, the horses?" returned Ned.

"I hope they do," laughed the guide. "No; Master Walter means Bud Stevens and the gang. Find us? Why, those fellows could trail a cat across the Desert Maze if they happened to take a notion to do so."

There being plenty of dry stuff about, the boys built up a blazing camp-fire as soon as night came on. Gathering about it they told stories and sang songs.

"I move that Stacy Chunky Brown favor us with a selection," suggested Ned. "He has a very rare voice—an underdone voice some might call it."

"Yes, Chunky," urged Walter. "You haven't sung for us since we started."

"Me? I can't sing. Besides it might scare the wild horses," protested Stacy.

"I guess there's no doubt about that. But we'll take the chances."

"Yes, do sing, Chunky," added Walter. "It may soften Ned's hard heart."

Stacy cocked an impish eye at Ned Rector.

"All right, I'll sing," decided the fat boy, clearing his throat.

"Stand up," thundered Ned. "Have some respect for the audience."

Stacy stood up.

"What are you going to favor us with?" questioned Tad.

"It's a little thing of my own," grinned Stacy. "Hope you'll like it."

"Oh, we'll like it all right," chuckled Ned. "The audience will please refrain from applauding until the performer finishes."

"What's the name of the piece?" demanded Walter.

"Hasn't been named. You can name it if you wish."

"Go ahead, go ahead. Never mind the name," chorused the lads.

Stacy surveyed the upturned, laughing faces of his companions and then launched out in a shrill soprano:

> It's all day long on the alka-li,
> Where the coyotes howl and the wells run dry,
> Where the badgers badge in the water holes,
> And the twisters twist the old tent poles—
> Right up from the alka-li.

"Yeow!" shrieked the Pony Rider Boys.

"It's a new poet. Hurrah for the poet lariat!" shouted Ned Rector, jumping up and down, slapping his thighs in his amusement.

"Go on, give us another verse," laughed the guide. "That's real po'try that is."

"Is there another verse?" cried Walter.

Chunky nodded solemnly.

"Hush! He is going to sing some more," cautioned Tad Butler, holding up his hand for silence.

"Ahem," began Stacy. Throwing back his head he began again:

> When the wind blows high o'er the Desert Maze,
> And sand in your eyes interferes with your gaze,
> Then the Pony Rider Boys they lose their pants;
> Don't dare sit down for fear of the ants —
> That hide in the alka-li.

Stacy sat down blinking, solemn as an owl. But if he was solemn his companions were quite the opposite. The boys formed a ring about him, and between their yells of appreciation, began dancing around in a circle shouting out in chorus the last two lines of the second verse:

> Don't dare sit down for fear of the ants —
> That hide in the alka-li.

Professor Zepplin and Tom Parry were laughing immoderately, but their voices could not be heard above the uproar made by the joyous Pony Riders. No such carnival of fun probably ever had disturbed the foothills of the San Antonio range, nor extended so far out over the maze of the great Nevada Desert.

"Sing it again! Sing it again!" commanded the boys.

They hauled the protesting Chunky to his feet, stood him on a box of pickled pigs' feet, compelling him to begin the song all over again.

"It's all day long on the alka-li.
Where the coyotes howl and — —"

"Ki-i-i-i-o-o-o! Ki-i-i-i-o-o-o-ki! K-i-i-i-o-o-ki!"

A long wailing sound — a dismal howl, suddenly cut short the joyous ditty.

"What's that!"

"Ki-i-i-i-o-o-o! Ki-i-i-i-o-o-ki!"

"Coyotes," laughed the guide.

There seemed to be hundreds of them. From every peak in the range their mournful voices were protesting.

All at once out in the black maze of the desert another bunch of them began their weird wailing.

"We're surrounded," announced the Professor.

"Shall we get the guns?" asked Walter.

"No, they're expressing their indignation at Chunky's song," jeered Ned.

"Let 'em howl. I don't care. If they don't stop I'll sing some more," threatened the fat boy.

# CHAPTER XIV
## FUN IN THE FOOTHILLS

The Professor found difficulty even in driving the lads to their beds that night. When they did finally tumble in and pull the blankets over them they were unable to sleep, between the howling of the coyotes and their laughter over Stacy Brown's new-found talent.

"They'll go away when the moon comes up," called the guide when the boys protested that the beasts kept them awake.

"Why can't we shoot at them?" asked Stacy.

"It will alarm the wild horses," said the guide. "We don't want to chase them off the range. Neither would the horse-hunters like it if we were to begin shooting."

"Go to sleep!" commanded the Professor.

Then the boys settled down. After a time the moon came up, but instead of quieting the coyotes it seemed to have urged them on to renewed efforts. They grew bolder. They approached the camp until a circle of them surrounded it.

Out of Stacy Brown's tent crept a figure in its night clothes. It was none other than Stacy himself. In one hand he held a can of condensed milk that he had smuggled from the commissary department that afternoon.

He wriggled along in the shadow of a slight rise of ground until he had approached quite near the beasts. He could see them plainly now and Stacy's eyes looked like two balls.

The animals would elevate their noses in the air, and, as if at a prearranged signal, all would strike the first note of their mournful wail at identically the same instant.

Suddenly the figure of the Pony Rider Boy rose up before them, right in the middle of one of the unearthly wails.

"Boo!" said Stacy explosively, at the same time hurling the can of condensed milk full in the face of the coyote nearest to him.

His aim was true. The can landed right between the eyes of the animal. The coyote uttered a grunt of surprise, hesitated an instant, then, with tail between his legs, bounded away with a howl of fear.

"Yeow! Scat!" shrieked the fat boy.

The whole pack turned tail and ran with Stacy after them in full flight, headed for the desert.

Tom Parry, aroused by this new note in the midnight medley, tumbled out just in time to see Stacy disappearing over the ridge. The guide was followed quickly by the other three boys of the party and Professor Zepplin.

"Hey, come back here!" shouted Parry.

The fat boy paid no attention to him. He was too busy chasing coyotes across the desert at that moment to give heed to anything else.

"Get after him, boys! If he falls they're liable to pile on him and chew him up before we can get to him!" commanded the guide.

Over the ridge bounded the pajama brigade. The coyotes, frightened beyond their power of reasoning, if such a faculty was possessed by them, were now no more than so many black streaks lengthening out across the desert.

The lads set up a whoop as they started on the chase after their companion.

"Rope him, somebody!" shouted Parry.

"Haven't any rope," answered Tad, with a muttered "Ouch!" as his big-toe came in contact with the can of condensed milk.

Laughing and shouting, they soon came up with Stacy, however, because he could not run as fast as the other boys. Tad caught up with him first, and the two lads went down together. In another minute the rest of the party had piled on the heap.

"Get up!" shouted Tad. "Somebody's standing on my neck."

"Yes, and—and you've pushed my face into the desert," came the muffled voice of Chunky Brown.

Laughing and all talking at once, the knot was slowly untied. Two of them grabbed the fat boy under the arms, while a third got between the lad's feet and picked them up, much as one would the handles of a wheelbarrow. In that manner they triumphantly carried Stacy back to the camp.

Reaching his tent, they threw the fat boy into his bed.

The tall, gaunt figure of the Professor appeared suddenly at the tent entrance. Some of the boys darted by him, the others crawling out under the sides of the tent, all making a lively sprint for their own quarters.

"Young men, the very next one who raises a disturbance in this camp to-night is going to get a real old-fashioned trouncing. Not having any slipper, I'll use my shoe. Do you hear?"

Not a voice answered him, but as he strode away the moon-like face of Stacy Brown might have been seen peering out at him. Quiet reigned in the camp of the Pony Rider Boys for several hours after that. Yet they were destined not to pass the night without a further disturbance, though the Professor did not use his shoe to chastise the noisy ones.

It lacked only a few hours to daylight when the second interruption occurred. And when it arrived it was even more startling than had been the fat boy's chase of the cowardly coyotes.

There was a sudden sound of hoof-beats.

"Ki-yi! Ki-yi!" shrieked a chorus of voices.

A volley of shots was fired as an accompaniment to the startling yells. A moment later and a body of horsemen dashed into camp, which they had easily located by the smouldering camp-fire.

The Pony Rider Boys were out of their tents in a twinkling.

"Wow!" piped Stacy.

Bang! Bang!

Two bullets flicked the dirt up into his face. Bud Stevens and his companions were in a playful mood again.

"Hey, you! Better look out where you're shooting to!" warned Stacy.

Bud let go another volley.

"The Professor'll take you over his knee and chastise you with his shoe, if you don't watch sharp," said Stacy.

"Come out of that. Where's the kiddie? I want to see my kiddie!" laughed Bud Stevens.

By this time, with his companions, he had dismounted, turning the ponies loose to roam where they would. The whole camp, aroused by the shouting and shooting, had turned out after pulling on their trousers and shoes. Tom Parry, piling fresh fuel on the embers of the camp-fire, soon had the scene brightly lighted. There was no more sleep in camp that night. Professor Zepplin accepted the new disturbance with good grace.

"We're going to eat breakfast with you," Bud Stevens informed them.

"That's right. What we have is free," answered the Professor hospitably.

"That's what I was telling the bunch," nodded Bud. "Our chuck wagon'll be along when it gets here. We've got a schooner with six lazy mules toting it down along the edge of the foothills. If it ever gets here we'll stock you up with enough fodder to last you the rest of your natural lives."

"A schooner, did you say?" questioned Stacy, edging closer to the cowboy.

"Yep; schooner."

"Where's the water?"

"Say, moon-face, didn't you ever hear tell of a prairie schooner!"

Chunky shook his head.

"Well, you've got something coming to you, then," replied Bud, turning to the others again.

"When do you start your horse-hunt? I presume that's the purpose of your visit here?" asked the Professor.

"Yep. Soon as the wagon gets here with the trappings. After breakfast we'll look around a bit. Been some of them through here to-day, I see."

"Yes, how did you know that!" questioned Tad.

"We crossed the trail just at the edge of the camp here when we came in. Didn't you see them?"

"We saw one of them and the tracks of the rest — —"

"Yes, we — we — we saw the white horse — —"

"The Angel?" demanded Bud, interested at once.

"I don't know whether you'd call it an angel or not. It struck me that it was quite the opposite," laughed Tad. "It was a white stallion, and when I got in its way it just bowled me over and rolled me down the hill — —"

"The white stallion, fellows," nodded Bud. "I told you so. Come along, kiddie, and show me that trail. I'll tell you in a minute if he's the one."

Tad took the horse-hunter to the trail that he had followed up the mountain side. Bud lighted match after match, by the light of which he ran over the confusion of hoofprints. Finally he paused over one particular spot, and with a frown peered down upon it.

"That's him. That's the Angel," he emphasized.

"Why do you call him that?"

"Because of two things," answered Bud. "First place, he's white. That's the color angels is supposed to be, most of 'em says. Then, if you'll look at his hoof-mark, you'll see the frog is shaped like a heart. More angel. Then again — that's three times, ain't it? — he's got a temper like angels ain't supposed to have."

"So I have observed," agreed Tad, with a laugh.

"And that's why we call him the Angel. We'll get the old gentleman this time or break every cinch strap in the outfit."

There was rejoicing among the horse-hunters when they heard that it was indeed the Angel himself whose trail they had come upon.

"He's got the finest bunch of horse flesh with him that you'll find anywhere on the desert," averred another. "Old Angel won't travel with any scarecrows in his band. He's proud as a peacock with a new spread of tail feathers."

"S'pose you don't know how many there are in the band, eh, kiddie?" questioned Bud.

"Twenty-one and a colt," answered Tad promptly.

"Oho! So — but Tom Parry told you, of course."

"Tom Parry didn't," objected the guide. "Master Tad read the trail himself."

"Shake," glowed Bud, extending his hand to Tad. "You're the right sort for this outfit. We'll let you help point the bunch into the corral when we get them going. You'll see stars before you get through with that job — stars that ain't down on the sky-pilot's chart."

"It won't be the first time, Mr. Stevens. I've seen enough of them to make a Fourth of July celebration, already."

Just after breakfast, to which the camp had sat down at break of day, the horse-hunters began their preliminary work. Bud directed two of his men to work south, two more to ride north, while he would take the center of the range.

"What I want," he explained to the boys, "is to find where the wild horses are waterin' these days. They've been around these parts for more than two weeks, so we know they've got a nice cold water hole somewhere."

"What were they doing on the desert?" asked Walter. "I thought they had just come across."

"No; they were out for a play. That shows they had had plenty to eat and drink. Professor, I think I'll take the kiddie along with me," announced Bud, much to Tad's surprise, and, judging from the expression of the lad's face, pleasure, as well.

Professor Zepplin glanced at the guide inquiringly. Parry nodded his head.

"He'll be all right."

"Yes, you may go, Tad. But be careful. Don't let him get into any difficulties, Mr. Stevens. He's a venturesome lad."

"Guess he's able to wiggle out of anything he gets into," grinned the horse-hunter. "Come along; take a hunch on your cinch straps, a chunk of grub in your pocket; then we're ready to find where the Angel washes his face every morning and night."

Tad lost no time in getting ready for the trip to trail the wild horses to their lair, and in a few moments the horse-hunters rode from the camp, followed by the envious glances of the Pony Rider Boys.

"Wish I were going along," muttered Chunky ruefully, as he turned his back on them and gazed off across the desert.

# CHAPTER XV
# BUD PROMISES SOME EXCITEMENT

The horse-hunter and his young companion laid their course at right angles to the reach of the range.

The trail rose slowly to pass between low buttes, leading on under the great spreading Joshua trees that capped the range itself. Off to the east and south of them, plainly exposed to view, lay the yellow stretch of the Ralston Valley that went on and on until it eventually terminated in Death Valley. The dry lake beds in the desert, looked, with the sun shining on them, like great pearls set in the Desert Maze. Tad thought they were water, but Bud Stevens informed him that they were filled with water only after a heavy thunderstorm, or in the early spring.

"You ought to have come down here earlier in the season," he told the lad. "It's a pretty bad time to cross the desert now."

"Yes, we know that. But we are not looking for easy trips," laughed the lad.

As they moved slowly along, the cowboy horse-hunter explained many of the secrets of the trail to his young companion, as well as describing horse-hunts in which he had taken part in the past.

"But I don't understand why they have come all the way across the desert to get into this range?" said Tad. "Why did they not remain on the other side where, I understand, there is plenty of forage?"

"It's a peculiar thing, kiddie, but hosses, wild or tame are like human beings in some ways. They like to get back home."

"What do you mean?"

"Wild horses always will go back to the range where they were born. Sometimes they run away from the range ahead of a storm; sometimes they are captured and taken away. But if they ever get the chance, back they go to the place where they were born. Angel was born in this range, and so were most of the mares and others that have come over with him. When a halfbreed Cherokee came into camp and told us the band of horses was seen stretched out on the mesa on the other side, I knew they were getting ready to hike across the desert, so we prepared to come here."

Tad was listening intently. All this was new to him and much of it not entirely understandable.

"Did you ever notice how animals act before a big storm?" asked Bud.

"No; I can't say that I have."

"Next time you see a lot of horses stretched out on the ground on their sides, heads close to the ground, all looking as if they were asleep, you'll know there's a big storm coming."

"Why do they do that?"

"I don't know, unless it is to rest themselves thoroughly before running away from the storm that they know is coming."

"How do they know a storm is coming, unless they can see it?" marveled the boy.

"Kiddie, you'll have to ask the horses. Bud Stevens don't know — nobody knows. A fellow with whiskers and wearing spectacles one of — of them scientific gents — told me once that it was a kind of wireless telegraph, that newfangled way of sending ghost messages. Said they got it in the air. Mebby they do; I don't know. They get it. Sometimes you'll see the colts running up and down. That's another sign of storm."

"That's strange. I never heard it before," mused the lad.

"And speaking of colts, did you ever know that sometimes a band of horses will take a great fancy to a frisky young colt?"

"No."

"Yes. They'll follow the colt for days, with their eyes big and full of admiration for the awkward critter. And they'll fight for him too. But 'tisn't often necessary, 'cause very few horses will bother a colt. Ever see a hoss fight?"

Tad admitted that he had not.

"Ought to see one. It's the liveliest scrimmage that you ever set eyes on. Beats that one back there on the desert, when you plunked me on my head in a water hole. Jimminy! but you did dump me proper," grinned the cowboy.

"Hope you don't lay it up against me," laughed Tad.

"No. Got all over that. I got what was coming to me—coming on the run. Say, got the trail on your side there? They seem to have shuffled over to the northward a bit."

"Yes, I'm riding on their footprints now."

"That's all right then. Don't want to let it get away from us."

"Where do you think they are heading, Mr. Stevens?"

"For the mesas up the range further. There's plenty of grazing there and there must be water close by. What we want to do, to-day, is to locate them and find out just where they go for their water. Then, when the schooner gets down to your camp, we'll haul our outfit up in the range and build a corral to drive them into."

"Do you always make a capture?"

"Us? No. Sometimes the leaders of the band are too smart for us. They beat us proper. Why, they're sharper than a Goldfield real estate man, and those fellows would make you believe an alkali desert was a pine forest."

"Look there!" interrupted Tad, pointing.

"What is it, kiddie?" demanded the horse-hunter, pulling up sharply.

"One of the horses, I think it must be the leader, seems to have left the trail here and started off at right angles."

Stevens rode over to the other side of Tad, and gazed down, his forehead wrinkling in a frown.

"Yes, that's the Angel. Don't know what he's side-tracked himself here for. He can't see far, so it was not an observation that he was about to take. He's either seen or scented something. Hold my pony while I take a look."

The cowboy dismounted, striding rapidly away with gaze fixed on the trail ahead of him. A few moments later he returned.

"Find anything?" asked Tad.

"The big one scented something, or thought he did."

"But where did he go?"

"Turned just beyond here and followed along the same way the others were going. You'll find his trail joining ours after we get on a piece. I'd like to know what he thought he smelled," mused Bud.

"I didn't know horses could scent a person or thing like that."

"What, horses? Wild horses have got a scent that's keener than a coyote's."

"There's the white stallion's trail again," exclaimed the lad.

Bud nodded. "Told you he'd come back."

For the next hour they rode along without anything of incident occurring, Tad constantly adding to his store of knowledge regarding mountain and plain. The lad was himself a natural plainsman and proved himself an apt pupil.

All at once Bud pulled up his pony sharply and studied the ground.

"What is it?" questioned Tad.

"We've struck luck for sure. Boy, I'll show you something that'll make your eyes stick out so you can hang your hat on them," cried the cowboy exultingly.

"You—you mean we have come upon the wild horses?" asked the lad.

"Yes, and more. Come this way and I'll show you. See this trail?"

Tad nodded.

"Well, it was made by another band of horses."

The announcement did not strike Tad as especially significant.

"They headed for the mesas, too?"

"Looks that way," grinned Bud. "And they're headed for trouble at the same time. There's going to be music in the air pretty soon, kiddie, and you and I want to be on hand to hear the first tune."

Tad gazed at him questioningly.

"This second bunch of horses is led by a big black stallion known to the hunters as Satan. He's up to his name too. He's one of the most vicious cayuses on the open range. Don't you see what this trail means?"

The lad confessed that he did not.

"It means that Satan is on the trail of the Angel. When Satan and the Angel meet there'll be the worst scrap you ever heard of, kiddie."

"Will they fight?"

"Will they fight?" scoffed Bud Stevens. "Guess you never saw two wild stallions mix it up."

"No."

"There's bad blood between Satan and the Angel and there has been for a long time. The black stallion has been on the white one's trail for more than a year. I don't know what it's all about, but I know that, if they come up with each other, there is going to be trouble. If they don't look out we'll bag the whole bunch. I wish our outfit was here. I suppose we ought to hustle back and get ready for the drive, but I'm going to see Satan and the Angel meet, if it's the last thing I ever do. Come on — we'll have to ride fast."

Putting spurs to their ponies, they set off at a fast pace over the uneven, rugged trail.

# CHAPTER XVI
# THE BATTLE OF THE STALLIONS

The trail grew hotter as they advanced.

"See, Satan's running now."

The pursuers increased their speed, although they could not hope to travel as rapidly as the black stallion and his followers. The wild horses' trot had by this time become leaps, as the followers could plainly see from the trail that had been left behind. Satan and his band were traveling in single file, their whole attention being centered on running down the Angel.

"Do you think Satan scented the others?" asked Tad, when they struck a level piece of ground so that they could relax their vigilance a little.

"No doubt of it at all. But he didn't know it was just then. He only knew it was a horse. He knows now that the other bunch is ahead of him."

"How do you know that?" queried Tad.

"By the trail," replied Stevens. "Don't you see, the Angel is going faster. They are both on a run now."

"Then the Angel must be afraid. Is that it?"

"Not much. He wants to find a better place in which to fight. This place is bad medicine for a horse battle. They're all heading for the mesas, just as I thought first."

The cowboy was leaning well forward in his saddle, eyes on the trail, instead of looking ahead. Tad, on the contrary, was straining his eyes, hoping to catch sight of the two bands of fleeing horses; but not a sign of them did he see. Bud was the first to inform him that they were nearing the object of their chase.

"Satan's going slower. He is coming up with the others. Let up a little, and don't talk in a loud tone. We don't want to disturb them nor let either of the bands get an idea they are followed. They might race off to some other part of the range. We want to catch them all later, if we can."

Their ponies were slowed down to a trot, with Bud Stevens leading.

All at once he held up his hand for a halt. Tad pulled up shortly.

"What is it? Do you see them?" he whispered.

Bud shook his head.

"Not yet. We're close to them, though. Jump off and tether your nag. We've got to go on afoot. They'll smell our ponies if we ride any further."

Moving rapidly, the man and the boy, led their mounts in among the trees, where they made them fast with the stake ropes. Then both started on a jog-trot along the trail.

"How far do we have to go do you think?"

"Don't know. Hope it's not far or we're liable to miss the show."

"I can run as fast as you can if you want to go faster."

"Hark! Hear that?" exclaimed Bud.

"Yes, what was it?"

"They're lining up for the battle. That was a stallion's scream of defiance. It is a challenge for battle. There goes the other one. That's the Angel telling Satan to come on and fight. Now Satan's answering him."

It was all just so much noise to Tad Butler. The meaning of the harsh sounds conveyed nothing to him, but to Bud Stevens they were full of meaning.

"Careful, now. We're getting near."

Both men sped along as fast as their feet would carry them, but without making a sound that might have been heard a dozen yards away.

"Hist!" warned Bud, crouching low.

Grasping his companion by the arm, he crept to the right, finally emerging from behind a rise of ground which had shielded their progress.

"Look there," he whispered.

Tad looked. Below him lay a broad, open mesa, its upper end within a stone's throw of where he stood. But that was not what attracted his attention. A band of horses of many colors and sizes stood arrayed on each side of the little plain.

Advanced a few yards from the band on the right, was a magnificent black stallion, pawing the earth and uttering shrill challenges. On the other side of the field was the Angel. He was not pawing the earth. Instead he was standing proudly, his curving neck beautifully arched, his pink nostrils distended and held high.

"What a wonderful animal!" said Tad under his breath. "And that black! I can understand why he is called Satan. What are they going to do?"

"Fight! Don't you understand? They're getting ready to settle their old score, and a merry mix-up it'll be," replied the cowboy in a whisper.

"Yes, yes," breathed Tad, scarcely able to curb his excitement.

"There they go!"

With a wild scream Satan and the Angel bounded into the center of the field. As they neared it each swerved to his right and dashed by, avoiding his opponent.

"Act as if they were afraid of each other," said Tad.

"They're not. They're trying each other out—sparring for an opening as it were. You'll see in a minute."

The fighters returned to the charge. They did not flinch this time. With a rush they came together, rearing in the air, jaws wide apart. Their fore-feet struck out. Both stallions broke, wheeled and kicked viciously.

Neither had landed a blow.

Next time they came at each other walking on their hind feet. They were sparring with their fore feet like fighters in the ring, their hoofs making such rapid thrusts that the eye could scarcely follow them. Satan reached for the head of his antagonist with a quick sweep. The white stallion blocked the blow cleverly.

**They Were Sparring with Their Fore Feet like Fighters in the Ring.**

Yet, in doing so, he had left an opening. Satan took instant advantage of it. The black stallion's head shot forward. It reminded Tad of a serpent striking at its victim.

"Ah! He landed!" exclaimed the cowboy.

A fleck of crimson on the creamy neck of the Angel showed where the vicious teeth of the black stallion had reached him. Yet, no sooner had the wound been inflicted than the Angel whirled. It was like a flash of light.

A white hoof shot out catching the black on the side of the head, sending him staggering to his haunches.

The white animal was upon him with a scream of triumph. Just as it seemed that the Angel was about to run him down, the black sprang to his feet, leaping to one side, and as the Angel passed, the hind hoofs of Satan were driven into his side.

The Angel uttered a cry of pain; it was returned by one of triumph from his antagonist.

"Oh, what a pity to see two such magnificent animals seeking to kill each other! Do you think one of them will be killed, Mr. Stevens?"

"They may. You can't tell. Hope there won't be a knock-out, 'cause we want both of those fellows and we'll get them too. I tell you, we're in luck this trip. We'll make a haul that will be worth a few thousand dollars, you bet. There they go again."

Changing their method of attack, the fighters began rushing, whirling, kicking and so timing their blows that their hind feet met with a crash that might have been heard a long distance away. The shiny coat of the black did not show that he had been wounded, but the watchers knew he had, for they had seen the teeth of the white animal buried in his side at least once.

A vicious charge of Satan's, threw the Angel from his feet. He struck the hard ground with a mighty snort, but was on his feet in an instant, returning to the charge, mouth open, feet pawing the air.

The two men could see the eyes of the desperate antagonists fairly blaze, while their shrill cries thrilled Tad through and through. Never in his life had he gazed upon such a scene—two giants of the equine world engaged in mortal combat. It was a scene calculated to make the blood course more rapidly through the veins of the boy, who, himself, possessed so much courage. And it did, in this case, though as a lover of horses his heart was filled with pity for the one who was to lose the battle. As yet there was no indication as to which this would be. They seemed equally matched, and thus far honors had been about even.

"Think the black can whip him?" he asked.

"Don't know, kiddie. I'll make a bet with you; take your choice."

"Thank you, I don't bet," answered the lad. "If I did, I couldn't bring myself to lay a wager on those two beautiful creatures that are trying to kill each other. Ah! There goes the black flat on his back!"

Before Satan could rise, the hoofs of the white one had been driven against him with unerring aim. Yet, the blow while it must have hurt, served to assist Satan to roll over. As a matter of fact he was kicked over, and thus helped to spring to his feet.

Each animal fastened his teeth in the flanks of the other at the same instant, and, when they tore themselves apart, each was limping.

On each side of the field the other members of the two bands of horses, stood stolidly observing the conflict. Neither side made an effort to participate in the battle.

Here and there a colt would break away and gambol out into the field, only to be recalled by a sharp whinny from its mother.

"It's queer they do not take a hand," marveled Tad.

"No; they never do. They look to their leader to fight their battles for them. When the battle is ended you will notice something else that will interest you."

"What?"

"You'll see when the time comes. Now watch them go at it."

And they did. It appeared as if each of the combatants was determined to put a quick end to the conflict. There was no lost time now. It was give and take. Blow after blow resounded from their hoofs. Now, one of the contestants would stagger and fall, only to be up and at his adversary, while their lithe, supple bodies flashed in the bright sunlight till the watchers' eyes were dizzy from following their rapid evolutions.

"I wish the boys might see this," breathed Tad, fascinated by the sight in spite of himself.

"So do I," grinned Bud.

"Did you ever see a battle of this kind?" asked the lad.

"Not like this. I've seen stallions fight, yes, but never such a scrap as this. Looks as if they'd be fighting all day. But they won't."

"Why not? They seem as strong as when they began."

"They are, but they're getting careless. They're taking longer chances every round. First thing you know, one of them will get kicked into the middle of next week. Whoop! That was a dandy!"

The Angel had planted both hind hoofs fairly on the side of Satan's head.

Satan had gone down. But when the white stallion made a leap, with the intention of springing upon his prostrate victim, the black rolled to one side, and in a twinkling had fastened his teeth upon his adversary's leg.

Only for a brief second did he cling there, then throwing himself out of the way sprang to his feet. The two animals met with a terrific crash, head-on.

Biting, kicking, screaming out their wild challenges of defiance the battle waxed hotter, faster and more furious.

The mares in the herds showed signs of uneasiness. They might have been observed tossing their heads and shifting almost nervously on their feet, but making no effort to move away or out into the field.

"Are the mares getting excited?" asked Tad in wonder.

"No. They see one of the stallions is going to get his knock-out in a minute."

"Which one?"

"I don't know."

"But how can they tell that, if we are unable to see either one of them weakening?"

"More ghost telegraphy, I guess," answered Bud, not for an instant removing his gaze from the fascinating scene before him. He, too, was becoming excited. He could scarcely restrain himself.

All at once, despite his caution, Bud Stevens uttered a whoop.

"The black's got him!"

"No, the Angel's got him!" shouted Tad Butler excitedly.

"No, he hasn't! It's the black, I tell you. See! There, he's kicked the Angel halfway across the mesa."

Now it was the Angel's turn to do some kicking. He did, and with terrific effect. Both hind hoofs were planted in the black's abdomen. Not once, but again and again. Yet the black was not thus easily defeated. With the sledge-hammer blows raining all over him, he struggled to his feet, and, with a desperate lunge, fastened himself upon the neck of his adversary.

Back and forth struggled the black and the white now, like a pair of wrestlers.

"Now, who do you think's got him, hey?" laughed Bud. "Why, the black'll eat his head off."

"I said Angel was going to win, and I think he is," retorted Tad. The white with a mighty toss of his powerful neck, threw Satan off, the fore feet of the Angel smiting and knocking Satan down.

Then followed a series of Gatling-gun-like reports as the Angel's hind hoofs beat a tattoo on the head of his prostrate victim.

The black was conquered.

Satan had been knocked out by the Angel, in the greatest equine battle that human eyes ever had gazed on.

"Aren't you glad I don't bet?" laughed Tad, his eyes flashing with the excitement of it all.

"I'd been willing to lose on that fight," grunted the cowboy.

"Is he killed, do you think?" asked the lad.

"No; he's just dizzy after the wallops he got on the head. You'll see him get up in a minute."

The Angel had backed off a few paces and there he stood, head erect, waiting as motionless as a statue until the moment when his fallen adversary should rise, if at all.

Slowly the black pulled himself to his feet. His head came up. He eyed the now calm white stallion half hesitatingly.

The watchers fairly held their breath, for it was a dramatic moment.

"They're going to fight again," muttered Tad.

"He's licked! He's got enough!" exclaimed Bud.

The black turned his back upon the white stallion, and with lowered head, dejection and humiliation apparent in every line, every movement of his body, walked slowly back to his own band.

The Angel followed at a distance, almost to the lines of the enemy. Then he paused, galloped back to the center of the field, and throwing up his head uttered a long, shrill scream of triumph.

One by one the mares of Satan's band detached themselves from his ranks, and, with their colts, trotted across the field to join the Angel's band.

# CHAPTER XVII
# ON A WILD-HORSE HUNT

A corral, constructed partially of brush on its wing ends, and of canvas for the corral proper, had been erected in one of the wide sage-covered draws of the San Antonio range. Across the opening of the corral, which resembled a pair of great tongs, the distance was fully half a mile.

Bud Stevens had decided to place the trap for the wild horses here in this open space in preference to laying it in the mountains. There was more room for operations in the open, he said.

Then again, the wild horses, as he knew from personal observation, were strong and full of fight.

"I guess we'll have to tire them all out before we can hope to get them in the corral," he told his men after they had finished their work of preparation.

The wagon with the horse-hunters' outfit had driven in late on the night following the battle of the stallions, and early next morning the horse-hunters, accompanied by the Pony Rider Boys and their own party, started out to make camp in the mountains, where they were to remain while the hunt lasted.

The battle which Tad and Bud had seen furnished a fruitful topic for discussion, and the two were kept busy relating the story of the fight until long after midnight.

But, while watching the battle, Bud Stevens had not lost sight of the object, of his trip into the mountains. He had calculated exactly where the stock had found a mountain spring, and it was from that point that the hunters were to start the animals on their trip to the corral.

The plan of operation was laid out with as much care and attention to details as a general would employ in planning a battle. The Pony Rider Boys were to participate in the chase. They could scarcely wait for the moment to arrive when they would be given an opportunity to show their horsemanship.

In the camp in the mountains they were told with great detail just what they were expected to do.

"I think you had better leave Chunky at home," warned Ned. "He'll stampede the whole bunch just as you are ready to drive them into the corral."

Chunky protested loudly.

"Guess I can stick on a pony as well as you can," he retorted.

"I'll vouch for that," smiled Tom Parry.

"He'll do," decided Bud. "Now, you fellows are all to string out in single file, following me until we have circled the herd. We should have them pretty well surrounded by noon. At that time they'll be at the spring filling up. When I'm ready to close in, I'll fire a shot. Each of you will fire in turn so that every one in line may be notified. If the critters refuse to drive, then we'll have to whip them into a circle and tire them out. But first, we must get them out on the open, no matter which way they go, then work them into the draw as fast as we can."

The horse-hunters nodded. They understood perfectly what they were expected to do. And the boys were to be scattered among the men at intervals instead of traveling together. It seemed very simple to them, but they were to learn that wild-horse hunting was a man's task.

"Are we allowed to rope if we get the chance?" questioned Tad.

"Not during the run. Of course, if you see an animal escaping after we have rounded them up, and you can do so without losing any of the others, rope if you want to. I reckon you'll have your hands full if you try it," concluded the horse-hunter.

"Are you going out, Professor?" smiled the guide.

"No, thank you. I think I shall remain close to camp and collect geological specimens. The boys will get into just as much trouble if I go with them as they would were I to remain at home. I suppose there is more or less peril in these wild hunts?"

"Yes, it's going some," laughed Bud. "But I guess none of them will get very badly knocked out if they obey orders and don't get in the way of a stampede. Those wild critters won't stop for nothing."

A scout came in late with the news that the herd was less than five miles from where the hunters' camp was located.

"That makes it all the easier. We'll start at daylight," said Stevens. "The plans will work out just right. Now you'd better all turn in and be ready for the hurry call in the morning."

Next morning all ate breakfast before the first hot wave trembled over the crest of the mountains across the broad desert. There was bustle and excitement in the camp.

When ponies had been saddled, ropes coiled and final preparations made, Bud Stevens looked his outfit over carefully, nodded his head and mounted.

"You boys don't want to do any shouting after we get out on the trail, you understand," he said. "We have to work quietly until we get them surrounded; then you may make all the racket you want. The more the better."

The Pony Riders nodded their understanding of the orders, and the company of horsemen set out across the mountains.

They made a wide detour so as not to alarm any of the stragglers who might not have followed the main body of horses to the watering place for their noon drink. A careful examination of the trail showed that the Angel and his band, as well as Satan and his few faithful followers, were well within the circle.

"We've got the whole bunch inside," exulted Bud, turning to Tad. "Now, boy, do your prettiest. We want to bag 'em all. If we do, I'll make you a present of any horse in the outfit."

"How about the Angel?" questioned Tad, with a twinkle in his eyes.

Bud hesitated.

"What Bud Stevens says goes," replied the cowboy. "The one who catches the stallion on these hunts, however, usually has the right to keep him if he wants to. If you want the Angel you've got to rope and take him after we get them rounded up."

"No, I wouldn't do anything like that," laughed Tad. "If I catch the Angel I'll make you a present of him."

At twelve o'clock, by the watch, they had completed the circle, or rather three-quarters of a circle, about the band of wild horses, leaving an opening toward the broad draw where the hidden corral had been located to trap the unsuspecting wild animals.

Stevens drew his gun, and, holding it above his head, fired two shots.

The signal was answered, almost instantly, by two shots some distance to their rear. Like the rattle of a skirmish line, guns popped in quick succession, the sounds growing further and further away as they ran down the long, slender line of horsemen to the eastward.

"Close in!" commanded the leader quietly. "Ride straight ahead; never mind me. I shall move further on before I turn. Good luck. Don't try to get in the way of a stampede. You can't stop them if they try it altogether."

"I'll look out," smiled Tad. Then they separated.

Tad could not hear a sound, save the light footfalls of his own pony. The mountain ranges might have been deserted for all the disturbance there was about him.

He had ridden on some distance when a loud snort suddenly called his attention to the right and ahead of him. There stood the Angel, facing him angrily.

Tad was so surprised at the suddenness of the meeting that he pulled his pony up shortly. For a moment they stood facing each other, then the wild animal with a loud scream of alarm, turned and went crashing through the brush. From the sound, a few seconds later, the lad knew that the stallion had gathered his band and that they were sweeping away from him at a lively pace.

"Here's where I must get busy," laughed the lad, the spirit of the chase suddenly taking strong hold upon him.

He touched his pony lightly with the spurs, drawing in on the reins. The little animal leaped away, Tad uttering a shrill yell, to warn any of the other hunters who might be within reach of his voice, that he had started on the trail of the wild band.

He heard a similar cry far off to his right and knew that Bud Stevens had heard and understood.

"I believe they're coming back," said the lad, realizing that the sound of galloping was plainer than it had been a few moments before. "I wonder what I ought to do. I'm going to try to head them off if they come this way," he decided.

All at once he saw the wild horses first from behind a huge rocky pile. Uttering a series of wild yells and whoops, swinging his quirt and sombrero above his head, the lad rode straight at the herd, his pony seeming to enter into the full spirit of the fun.

To Tad's surprise the leader of the herd deflected to the northward, running along a line almost parallel to that which the boy was following. Tad pressed in the rowels of his spurs a little harder, uttering a chorus of shrill yells.

"They mustn't get through," he fairly groaned. "They shan't get through! No, not if I ride my head off!"

Suddenly a volley of shots sounded some distance ahead of him, followed by a series of yells as if the mountains were alive with savage redskins.

It was Bud Stevens. The wild herd had come upon him just as they were about to turn northward and dive into the fastnesses of the mountains. Observing him they turned slightly to the west and continued on their mad course.

"Good boy!" Bud shrieked. "Draw up on 'em! Draw up on 'em!"

Tad did. It was a race, but a most perilous one. To the boy it seemed as if the feet of his pony were off the ground most of the time, his run having merged into a series of long, curving leaps as it reached from rock to rock.

Down a steep slope suddenly plunged the herd. Tad saw the flying pony of Bud Stevens directly abreast of them. The lad, apparently feeling no fear, brought his quirt down sharply on the flanks of his mount. The pony hesitated, rose and took a flying leap fully ten feet down the mountain side before its feet braced sharply and thus saved pony and rider from plunging on over.

Now Tad was yelling at the top of his voice, as that seemed the proper thing to do under the circumstances.

The wild band was heading for the open, just as Bud Stevens had planned. But the fleeing horses were seeking to get out on the open plain where they might soon outdistance their pursuers.

Tad and his pony went down that rugged mountain side as if the pony were a mountain goat. The boy never had experienced such a thrilling ride, and the jolts he got made his head dizzy.

"M-m-my, this is going some!" he gasped.

Tad was shouting for pure joy now. When his mount landed on all fours among the foothills he was not more than two minutes behind Bud Stevens himself.

"Great! Great!" floated back the voice of the horse-hunter, who, turning in his saddle, had observed Tad's leaping, flying descent of the mountain.

Tad admitted to himself that this was riding, and he compared it with the day he first rode his own pony up the main street in Chillicothe, Missouri. That ride, at the time, seemed a very exciting one. Since then he had acquired more skill, else he never would have been able to shoot down the rugged mountain at almost express train speed.

They were now out on the desert prairie. Bud was trying to point the leaders in to send them to the southward. Now that Tad was on level ground he was able to put on more speed. Very slowly, indeed, his pony straightening out to its full length, he drew up on the racing herd.

"Guess I'd better not yell any more till I get abreast of them," he decided, which was good judgment, as Bud Stevens said to him afterwards.

"Lay back a little!" shouted Bud when the boy got too close. "They're liable to dodge behind me at any second and break through our line."

Tad slackened his speed, at which the wild band drew away from him almost as if he were standing still. Then, he put spurs to his mount again, and drew up abreast of the trailers.

At the head of the line the horse-hunter was fighting with the leaders, trying to turn them toward the place where the great corral was hidden.

Suddenly that which Bud Stevens had feared occurred. The white stallion's forefeet plowed the earth. Cowboy and pony shot by him, and the wily stallion slipped behind them. Followed by his band, the Angel headed off across the desert in the very direction that the hunters did not want him to go.

"Nail him!" bellowed Bud.

Tad needed no further command. Already his keen eyes had noted the move. Putting spurs to his pony he raced to the white stallion's side, leaving Bud far to their rear.

The Angel sought, in every way in its power, to shake off the boy who so persistently hung at its side. All at once the stallion reached over, fastening its teeth in the neck of Tad Butler's pony. Tad, however had been quick enough to foresee the move and had jerked his little mount to one side. Yet, he had not done so quickly enough to save the broncho from a slight flesh wound.

Slackening its speed, the Angel then made a vicious lunge at the lad's left leg, biting right through the heavy chaps with which his legs were protected.

The boy swung his quirt, bringing it down again and again on the stallion's pink and white nose, until the beast, unable to stand the punishment longer, uttered a snort, changing its course more to the southward.

"I've turned him! I've turned him!" shouted Tad.

He had accomplished what the leader of the horse-hunters had been unable to do.

Bud Stevens, far to the rear on the desert, tossed his sombrero in the air, uttering a long, far-reaching yell of approval.

# CHAPTER XVIII
## ROPED BY ROUGH RIDERS

Tad replied with an exulting yell.

The band of wild horses was headed toward the corral. Yet they refused to enter, just when they were upon the point of heading in between the hidden wings. Some instinct, it seemed, warned them to beware. The line straightened out, and a few minutes later the animals began racing in a circle four miles wide.

"I'm afraid my pony never'll be able to stand this grilling. But we'll keep going as long as we've got a leg left to stand on," laughed the plucky lad.

"Drop out and let me take a round with them. We've got to tire them out," shouted Bud, putting spurs to his pony and dashing up beside Tad.

The lad regretfully pulled his mount down to a walk, then rode out on the desert some distance, so as to be out of the way when the circle once more came his way.

"Guess it's just as well," he muttered. "The pony couldn't have stood up much longer. My, those wild animals can travel!"

A heavy coating of gray dust covered both boy and horse, except where here and there the gray was furrowed with streaks of perspiration. Tad gave his mount the reins, and sat idly watching the cloud of dust rolling over the desert, showing where Bud Stevens was driving the wild-horse band in an effort to tire them, so that they might be easily headed into the great corral.

They soon swept by Tad, and on out over white alkali desert once more.

On the next round Bud motioned to Tad to take up his end of the relay.

"Give it to 'em. Drive 'em till they can't stand up!" bellowed Bud.

But the lad scarcely heard the horse-hunter's voice. Already he had been swallowed up in the great yellow cloud and was riding hard by the white stallion.

Discovering that he had another rider beside him, the Angel made a desperate effort to run the lad and his pony down that he might break the line and head off to the northwest. Tad beat him over the nose with his quirt again, and the stallion promptly changed its mind, for the pink nose was still tender from the drubbing Tad had given it a short time before.

"The men are lining up for a drive," warned Stevens when the herd thundered by him again. "I'll keep behind you. We're going to try to drive them in this time. They're weakening fast."

"You want me to hold the leader?" asked the boy.

"Yes. Keep him up. Don't give him a second's leeway. The rest will follow him; don't worry about them."

"Where are the other fellows?"

"Over to the east. They're hiding until the herd gets close enough; then they'll appear, raising a big noise. That's the time you and I will have our hands full."

"Strikes me our hands have been pretty full," answered the lad, his face wrinkling into a forced grin.

Bud Stevens slackened the speed of his pony, dropping back and disappearing in the dust cloud.

"After all, I guess the other fellows will have the hardest work," mused the lad. "They've got to stop the rush while all I have to do is to keep on going, following that big, white stallion. I wish I could rope him, but I guess he would have the broncho and myself on our backs in no time."

Tad turned his attention to the work in hand. He did not know just where the other horse-hunters were secreted, but his eyes were fixed on a low-lying butte some distance to the eastward. He saw no other place from which they could carry out the manoeuvre successfully.

Tad grew a bit anxious as the wild horses curved more and more to the eastward. In a few moments they would be too far to the left to permit of heading them toward the hidden corral.

"I guess they must be going to let us drive them around the circle once more," he decided, "No! There they come!"

With a yell, followed by a rattling fire of revolver shots, a dozen ponies shot from behind the low-lying butte. The horse-hunters hurled their bronchos right against the wall of fleeing animals.

Volley after volley was fired into the ground right under the very feet of the wild horses. Here and there a rider was unseated in a sudden collision in the dust cloud with a charging wild horse.

"They've turned them!" bellowed Bud Stevens.

The Pony Rider Boy now began to realize the truth of this, for the Angel came bounding toward him, crowding right up against the side of Tad's pony. Tad was using foot and quirt, yelling like a wild Indian to frighten the big, white stallion into keeping to the left.

So successful were his efforts that the animal did give way a little.

"I've headed him!" shouted the lad in wild glee. Never had he had such an exciting day as this one was proving itself to be. He gave no thought to the danger of the chase. And now that he heard and recognized the shouts of his companions he was spurred to even greater efforts than before. Why this post of honor had been given to him he did not know. But Bud Stevens was not far behind. Bud was ready to stop the stampede that he momentarily expected, but which did not come.

"Give way a little!" came the command.

Tad recognized that he had, in his enthusiasm, been crowding the white stallion a bit too much. He drew off a little, not, however, decreasing his speed.

Already the band of wild horses had entered the wide-spreading wings of the corral, but because of the dust that enveloped him, Tad was unaware of this. He continued at his same terrific pace, with the tough little broncho rising and falling under him as he fairly flew over the uneven ground.

The horse-hunters had fallen into a triangle formation with the apex to the rear. They were driving the wild horses before them, using their guns in what appeared to be a most reckless fashion, shouting as if the whole band had gone suddenly mad.

On down between the brush barriers, that were now apparently rising out of the ground, sped the frightened band of wild horses. The white stallion began to understand that they were trapped.

Angel whirled suddenly and made a desperate effort to take the back trail. Tad and his pony dashing down the slight incline like a projectile, hit the stallion broadside. The collision was so sudden that the lad had a narrow escape from being hurled over the head of his own pony. It was only the convulsive grip of legs to the broncho's side that saved him from a bad spill.

With quick instinct he brought his quirt down on the broad back of the Angel. Smarting under the stinging blow and the surprise of the collision the white stallion whirled about again, heading right into the yawning corral.

The lad was now in the very midst of the crowding, fighting animals. He was battling every whit as desperately as were they. Bud Stevens had fallen back. He knew Tad was somewhere ahead in the mix-up, but he was powerless to get to him at that moment, nor could his voice reach the lad.

It was then that the boy realized where he was.

"I'm in the corral!" he cried, discovering that he was hemmed in by the canvas walls of the main enclosure itself. "And I guess I'm in a mix-up that will be hard to get out of."

The wild horses were charging about, screaming with anger and fear, rearing, biting, kicking, bowling each other over in their desperate efforts to escape. On every side, they found themselves met by the canvas walls, which none thus far had had the courage to assail.

"There's the black stallion—there's Satan," cried Tad in surprise. "I didn't know he was here."

The black's eyes were gleaming with anger. His lost courage was slowly returning to him. Satan was now ready to give battle to man or beast. All at once he dashed straight at the canvas wall, rose to it and cleared it in a long, curving leap, his rear feet ripping the cloth down a short distance as the hoofs caught it.

The keen eyes of the white stallion were upon him. In another instant his glistening body had flashed over the enclosing walls.

"Oh, that's too bad!" groaned Tad.

At that moment half a dozen horsemen appeared in the enclosure; as if by magic they threw themselves across the opening made by the two stallions, and thus made an impassable barrier. Tad had seem them coming, and divined their purpose. A daring plan suddenly flashed into his mind.

With a shrill yell, he dug in the rowels of his spurs. The broncho, understanding what was wanted of him, rose to the canvas well, clearing it without so much as touching it with his hoofs.

But while this was going on another scene was being enacted just outside the barrier. A few horse-hunters had been sent around there to head off just such an attempt at escape as had been made. With them was Stacy Brown. He was sitting on his pony, rope in hand when Satan cleared the wall.

He saw the dark body of the stallion plunge over. Instinctively the fat boy rose in his stirrups. His lariat whirled twice over his head, then shot out.

It sped true to the mark, catching Satan by the left hind foot just as he was finishing his leap.

"Yeow!" yelled Chunky.

The black stallion ploughed the ground with his nose, as the boy took a quick hitch of the rope about his saddle pommel.

That was where Chunky came to grief once more. His pony's feet were jerked out from under it by the mighty lurch of Satan when he went down. Stacy Brown and his broncho were thrown flat on the ground in a twinkling. The lad's right leg was pinned under the pony, but the boy, with great presence of mind, held the rope fast to the pommel.

Ropes flew from all directions, now that the stallion was down. In a moment more they had Satan entangled in a maze of them. The horse-hunters were shouting and yelling in triumph at the fat boy's splendid capture. So busily engaged were they in subduing the black that, for the moment, they lost sight of the fact that the Angel, followed by Tad Butler on his broncho, had cleared the barrier too.

Nor did Tad give heed to them.

With rope unslung he was stretching through the foothills at a breakneck pace, on the trail of the Angel.

"There goes the Angel, with the kid after him!" bellowed a cowboy.

Three men leaped into their saddles and were off like a shot.

Tad Butler slowly, but surely, drew up on the racing stallion. The pursuers saw him unsling his rope, holding the coil easily at his side.

"He's going to cast," cried the cowboys in amazement that the slender lad would undertake alone to capture the powerful animal.

"He'll be dragged to death!" warned one.

"Don't try it, kiddie!" shouted another at the top of his voice.

A chorus of warning yells were hurled after the intrepid Tad, to all of which he gave no heed. His eyes were fixed on the flashing body of the white stallion ahead of him, every nerve tense for the shock that would come a moment later.

All at once the pursuers saw Tad's right arm describe the familiar circle in the air. Then his lariat squirmed out. The Angel, running ahead of the boy could not see the rope in time to dodge it. The loop of the lariat dropped neatly over his head and suddenly drew taut.

The proud stallion which for years had defied the skill of the wild-horse hunters, went down to an inglorious defeat. But he was up like a flash. Then began a battle between the slender Pony Rider Boy and wild stallion that is talked of among the wild-horse hunters of the desert to this day.

Three times had Tad thrown the Angel before the others caught up with him, the lad's arms being well-nigh pulled from his body in the terrific lunges of the fighting Angel.

The ropes of the cowboys reached out for the maddened animal the instant they were within reach.

Such a shout went up as had probably never been heard on the range before when finally they had the white fighter securely roped down.

The Pony Rider Boys had distinguished themselves this day.

Tricing up one of the stallion's forward legs, so that he hobbled along like a lame dog, the hunters started back to the corral, shouting, singing and firing their revolvers, with Tad Butler proudly sitting his broncho at the head of the procession.

Not an animal had escaped from the other hunters. It had been a magnificent round-up.

# CHAPTER XIX
# WINNING THEIR REWARD

The horse-hunters had bound the black and left him, while they entered the corral to assist in roping the rest of the herd that were dashing wildly about. Every time a rope swung above a broad-brimmed sombrero, and shot out, a wild horse came down.

"I fell in, but I got him," greeted Chunky Brown, triumphantly, as Tad Butler rode up to him.

Tad laughed heartily when he saw his companion, Stacy Brown, proudly sitting on the head of the angry, snorting black stallion.

"You did, indeed, Chunky. How did you ever do it?"

"Just like any other experienced man would," replied the fat boy, in an important tone. "We got them both, didn't we, Tad!"

"Yes."

"And we'll keep 'em, eh!"

"Oh, no, Chunky. We couldn't do that. These horses belong to the hunters. They spend a great deal of money in preparing to capture them. It would not be right for us to expect to keep these two. We've been well paid for our labor in the fun we have had. Don't you think so?"

"Well, yes," decided Stacy a little ruefully.

"Let's see if we can help them," concluded Tad, riding up to the edge of the corral.

"Orders?" he called, as soon as he could attract Bud Stevens' attention.

"Yes; you might ride around to the entrance and come in. You can help us rope and hobble the stock if you want to."

Tad did as directed. There was no sport of the range that he took a keener enjoyment in than he did in roping, and by this time there were few men who could handle a rope more skillfully than he.

Ned and Walter were assisting in guarding the narrow entrance to the canvas corral when Tad finally rode through, entering the enclosure, where the excited animals were charging back and forth and round and round.

Bud was sitting on his pony in the center of the milling animals, directing the operations. First the hunters would rope and throw an animal; then they would bind up one of the front legs at the elbow, after which the horse was released. When the animals had staggered about the enclosure a few times trying to throw off the leg-binders, they were quite willing to stand still and nurse their anger.

"Sail in, boy!" called Bud.

Tad picked out a little bay that was kicking and squealing, dodging every lariat that was thrown at it. His first shot missed. The lad coiled his rope deliberately.

"I'll see that you don't dodge me this time, Mr. Bay," Tad muttered, and began slowly following the animal about the ring. The instant the bay's head was turned away from him Tad let go the rope, and the next second the stubborn animal lay on its side, another cowboy having made a successful cast over its kicking hind legs the moment it struck the ground.

Tad released his rope, then started for another cast. So he went on from one to another, and with as much coolness as if he had been roping wild horses all his life.

After half an hour's work young Butler saw Bud motioning to him. Tad rode up. The boy was bare-headed, having lost his sombrero somewhere in the enclosure, and not having thought to look for it, even if he had realized its loss.

"Take a rest," directed the horseman.

"I'm not tired."

"Yes, you are, but you don't know it. First thing you know, you'll tumble off your pony with a bad case of heat knock-out. Your face is as red as a lobster. Too bad the stallions got away," added Bud, who had been so thoroughly occupied in the corral that he had given no heed to what had been taking place outside.

"Lost the stallions?" questioned Tad, elevating his eyebrows.

"Yes, Satan and the Angel."

"Why, Mr. Stevens, we didn't lose them."

"I know, we got them in the corral all right, but that isn't getting them. They always manage to give us the slip somehow."

Tad's eyes danced.

"Then you've got a surprise coming to you, Mr. Stevens. Both stallions are lying outside the corral at this minute, tied up so tightly that they won't get away again."

"What! You're joking."

"No, I'm not. I mean it," laughed the lad in high glee.

Bud bent a steady look upon the boy. He saw that Tad was speaking the truth.

"How did it happen, kiddie?"

"Chunky roped the black by one of its hind feet just as the animal was taking the jump. Chunky got a bad fall, but he held fast to the black till the others could get their ropes on it."

"Hurray!" shouted Bud, carried away by his enthusiasm. "But what about the Angel, eh? Get him too, did you say?"

"Yes."

"How?"

"I jumped the fence after him, and ran a race with him out into the foothills, where I managed to get my lariat over his head and pulled him down. We had quite a scrimmage, but I should have lost him if I hadn't had help. The boys came to my rescue just in time."

"Huh!" grunted the cowboy, observing his companion with twinkling eyes. "You've got anything roped and hobbled that I ever saw."

That was Bud's only comment at the moment, but it carried with it a world of praise, causing Tad to blush.

All the rest of the afternoon was devoted to securing the animals that they had captured. Not a horse had escaped. Shortly after sunset the task was completed and the horse-hunters gave utterance to their feelings in a series of triumphant yells.

In the meantime three of the men had been sent back to bring over the camp outfit, which, owing to the fact that it had to follow a round-about trail, did not get in until some time after dark. Ned and Walter had accompanied the men back to camp to assist in packing their own outfit, Tad and Stacy remaining to keep watch over the prizes that they had captured.

Dinner that night, though a late one, was an occasion of boisterous good-fellowship, the two happy Pony Rider Boys coming in for much good-natured raillery.

"Don't want to join us, do you, kiddie?" asked Bud quizzically.

"I'd like to, of course. But it is not possible," answered Tad.

"We'll be off in the morning with our stock, you know. Better come along. You'll dry up and blow away down on the desert. It's had medicine where you're headed for."

"We're used to taking our medicine," laughed Tom Parry. "You probably have noticed as much in the short time you've known our bunch."

"You bet I have," laughed Bud. "And you take it in big doses, too."

"Allopathic doses," interjected the Professor.

"Don't know what they might be," answered Bud. "Sounds as though it might be something hard to swallow, though."

This bit of pleasantry caused a general laugh. The fun continued until late in the evening. Next morning the camp was astir at an early hour.

The captured horses were found to be considerably subdued after being roped all night. Bud's first work in the morning, after breakfast, was to take the two stallions in hand. They were freed of their bonds, and after a battle during which nearly every member of the party had been more or less mauled by the spirited beasts, the horse hunters succeeded in saddling and bridling Satan and the Angel.

Bud Stevens rode them about in turn, to the delight of the Pony Rider Boys who had never seen such bucking.

"Let me ride now," begged Stacy, after Stevens had to some extent subdued Satan.

The horseman permitted the lad to take to the saddle, but no sooner had Chunky done so, than Satan hurled him clear over the corral. Chunky, nothing daunted, came back smiling and tried it again, this time with entire success. Satan did not again succeed in unseating him.

Tad mastered the Angel without being thrown, and amid the cheers of the cowboys, who shouted their approval of his horsemanship.

All was now in readiness for the start of the cowboy band and their great herd of horses. Stevens had directed his men to take the two stallions outside the corral and stake them down securely. Then the men began driving the rest of the captured stock from the canvas prison. At first the animals evinced an inclination to run away. But with one leg in a sling this was not an easy task, and the horsemen rounded up the bunch with little difficulty.

"Here, here!" cried Tad. "You're forgetting the stallions, Mr. Stevens. You've left them staked down out back of the corral."

"Have I?" grinned Bud. "What did you want me to do with them?"

"Take them with you, of course," answered Tad, as yet failing to understand the horse-hunter's plan.

"Don't you want them, kiddie?"

"Want them — want them?" stammered Tad.

"Yes. They're yours, yours and the fat boy's."

"Oh, no, no, Mr. Stevens! I couldn't think of such a thing."

"Master Tad is right," approved the Professor. "We have not the least claim in the world on those animals. We — —"

"Say, Professor, who's running this side show?" demanded Bud.

"Why — why, of course it's your hunt, but — —"

"All right then, seeing as it's my outfit, I've decided that I don't want the stallions. Look here! We'd have lost part of that bunch, at least, if it hadn't been for your kids. Master Tad alone saved the herd from scattering all over the Ralston Desert. No, sir, I'm getting off cheaply. The stallions belong to the boys, and that's all there is to be said. S'long everybody. Come up to Eureka on your way out, and if I don't cut the town wide open for you, my name ain't Bud Stevens."

With a wave of his sombrero, Bud put spurs to his mount and galloped away to join his companions, who had started the herd on its way to Eureka, where the animals were to be shipped East.

Tad and Stacy were too full of surprise to express their feelings.

# CHAPTER XX
## VISITED BY A HALO

The Pony Rider Boys turned again to the Desert Maze. A week had elapsed since Bud Stevens and his party had left them. One evening, after a hard day in the saddle, the guide was sitting thoughtfully in his tent, when Professor Zepplin entered.

"Sit down?" asked the guide.

"For a moment only," answered the Professor.

"Weather's fine to-night."

"Yes, even though we have no water to speak of. Do you consider our situation at all serious, Mr. Parry?"

"Same old story, Professor. Sage brush and alkali. Tanks full one day, dry the next. There's no accounting for the desert. Every time I get out of the Desert Maze, as somebody has called it, I chalk down a mark on the wall."

"I am beginning to understand that it does hold perils of its own," answered Professor Zepplin, thoughtfully.

"Traveling over the desert is no picnic—that's a fact. Got to take it as it comes, though. If we go dry one day, most likely we fill up the next, or the day after that. Don't pay to get down in the mouth and fret."

"Yes, I understand all that. But I don't wish to take any great chances on account of the boys."

"The boys?" Tom Parry laughed. "Don't you worry about them. Those boys would thrive where a coyote would die at sight of his own eternal starvation shadow."

The Professor shook his head doubtfully.

"Turn 'em loose on the desert and they'd swim ashore somehow. Especially young Butler. He's quiet—he doesn't say much, but when he gets busy there's something doing. For sheer pluck he's got it over anything I ever saw—like a circus tent. Well, don't lose any sleep worrying about water. We'll catch a drop or two of dew out of a cactus plant some of these nights. See you in the morning. Good night," concluded the guide, rising and knocking the ashes from his pipe on his boot heel.

They had been working slowly toward the Death Valley region, and water was becoming more and more scarce as they proceeded. Indeed, the problem of where to find sufficient water for their needs had become a serious one. For the last three days all the water holes that the guide had depended upon to replenish their supply had failed them. What lay before them none knew.

When the camp awakened, late the next morning, the guide was nowhere to be seen. His pony likewise had disappeared. But they did not trouble themselves over Parry's absence, knowing that he had not left them without good reason and with many a sharp joke at each other's expense proceeded to get the breakfast ready. They had just sat down to the table when Tom Parry came riding in, covered with dust.

"Morning, boys. Fine day," he greeted, with his usual inscrutable smile, which might indicate either good or bad tidings.

"Prospecting?" questioned Tad.

"Taking my morning constitutional. Going to be hot enough to singe the pin feathers off a bald-headed sage hen to-day," he informed them, slipping from his saddle. After beating a cloud of alkali dust from his clothes he joined the party at the breakfast table.

"Find any?" asked Tad, eyeing him inquiringly, for Tad had an idea as to the object of the guide's early morning ride.

"Nary," was the comprehensive reply. "Have to take a dry shampoo to-day, I reckon."

"I suppose there is no water in sight yet?" asked the Professor, he not having caught the meaning of the brief dialogue between Tad and Tom Parry.

"No, sir. Not yet. We'll be moving as soon as possible after breakfast. Better use sparingly what little water you have left in your canteens. You may need it before we strike another water hole," he advised.

As usual, however, the spirits of the Pony Rider Boys were in no way affected by the shortage of water. Time enough to worry when their canteens were dry. These days, Tad and Stacy were occupying all their spare time in working with the two stallions they had captured. The Angel, under Tad's kind but determined training, was advancing rapidly and already had been taught to do a few simple tricks. Stacy, on his part, was not doing quite so well with Satan. The latter, like his namesake, was inclined to be vicious, biting and kicking whenever the evil spirit moved.

Ahead, on all sides of them as the sun rose that morning, lay wide stretches of gray, dusty soil, blotches of alkali alternating with huge patches of scattering sage brush, with no living thing in sight.

Overhead burned the blue of a cloudless sky; about them the suffocating atmosphere of the alkali desert.

It was not a cheerful vista that spread out before the lads. The ponies, suffering for want of water, took up the day's journey with evident reluctance. With heads hanging low they dragged themselves along wearily, half in protest, now and then evincing a sudden desire to turn about and head for the mountains.

"What ails these bronchos?" grumbled Ned Rector.

"Guess they're afraid of heat prostration," replied Chunky. "Don't blame them. I'm half baked myself."

"Glad you know what ails you," laughed Ned. "You ought not to feel bad about that, seeing it's your natural condition."

As they plodded on the guide's eyes were roaming over the plain in search of telltale marks that would reveal the presence of that of which they were in most urgent need—water. The landscape, by this time, had become a white glare, and the blue flannel shirts of the Pony Riders had changed to a dirty gray as if they had been sprinkled with a cloud of fine powder.

Their hair, too, was tinged, below the rims of their sombreros, with the same grayish substance, while their faces were streaked where the perspiration had trickled down, giving them a most grotesque appearance.

"How do you like it, Chunky?" grinned Ned.

"Oh, I've seen worse in Chillicothe," answered the fat boy airily. "The dust in Main Street is worse because it's dirtier."

"Judging from the appearance of your face at this minute, I'm obliged to differ with you," interjected the Professor, his own grim, dust-stained countenance wrinkling into a half smile. "Do we take a rest at midday, guide?"

Parry shook his head.

"Think we'd better keep going. Only be worse off if we stop now. Hungry, any of you?"

Stacy made a wry face and felt of his stomach, which action brought a laugh from the others.

Just then Stacy stiffened, then uttered a loud sneeze that shook him to his very foundations, causing Satan to jump so suddenly that he nearly unseated his rider.

"Whew! Thought my head had blown off. Guess we're all getting the grippe," he grinned, as the others began sneezing.

"Alkali," answered Parry. "You'll like that and the sage brush taste in your mouth more and more as you get to know them better."

"Excuse me," objected Ned. "I prefer talcum powder for mine, if I've got to sneeze myself to death on something. What time is it?"

"Dinner time," answered Stacy promptly. "I'll take ice cream."

"Dry toast will be more in your line, I'm thinking," suggested Ned.

"Or a sandwich," added Walter humorously.

"Hurrah, fellows! Walt Perkins has cracked a joke at last!" shouted Ned.

"Yes, it was cracked all right," muttered Chunky maliciously.

"Put him out! Put 'em both out!" cried Ned and Tad, while Tom Parry's stolid face relaxed into a broad smile.

"It appears to me that you young gentlemen are very humorous to-day," laughed the Professor.

"It's dry humor, Professor," retorted Ned.

Tad unslung his lariat.

"I'll rope the next boy who dares say anything like that again," he threatened. "See, even the burros are ashamed. They're hanging their heads, they're so humiliated."

"I don't blame them. Mine's swimming from the heat," rejoined the guide.

"Say, what's that?" demanded Chunky, pointing ahead of him, with a half-scared expression on his face.

"I don't see anything," answered the other lads.

"Chunky's 'seeing things,'" suggested Ned.

The fat boy was pointing to a bright circle of light that hung over the desert some five feet from the ground, directly ahead of him. The peculiar thing about it appeared to be that the circle of light kept continually moving ahead of him, and at times he caught the colors of the rainbow in it.

Stacy looked intently, but the bright light hurt his eyes and he was forced to lower his eyelids a little. This made the circle seem brighter than before.

Now Professor Zepplin had discovered the peculiar thing.

"What is that—what does it mean, guide?" asked the scientist.

"That—that ring of light?" asked Parry.

"Yes."

"That is a halo, sir."

"A halo?" chorused the boys.

"Must be Chunky's then," suggested Walter.

"I agree with you," added Ned. "But I don't see what right he has to a halo."

"That particular halo is a very common thing in the Desert Maze," Tom Parry informed them. "It is caused by heat refraction, or something of the sort——"

"Yes, yes. Oh, yes, I understand," nodded the Professor. "I recall having heard of something of the kind in hot countries, and——"

"Is this a hot country?" asked Stacy innocently.

"No, you ninny; this is a section of Greenland that's been dropped down here by an earthquake or something," laughed Walter.

"You're mistaken. It was washed down by the flood," corrected Ned.

All this helped to pass away the hours as well as to make the boys forget their troubles for the time being. Perhaps the lads did not fully realize the extent of their predicament. Not so the guide, however. He knew that they must find water soon. Not many hours would pass before the stock, unable to stand the strain longer, would give out, leaving the party in a serious plight. They would then be without water, and without horses to take them to water. The wild stallions, however, were accustomed to going without drink for long periods at a time, so that they were doing much better than the rest of the stock.

Tom Parry reasoned that they would be able to go through that day and part of the next without fresh supply, and that no serious consequences would result from it. Beyond that, he did not attempt to forecast what the result would be.

Late that afternoon, without having informed his charges, Parry varied his course, turning more to the west of south, eventually picking up a copper colored butte that rose out of the desert. Reaching it at last, Parry dismounted, and, bidding the others wait for him, he climbed up the rocky sides of the miniature mountain, quirt in hand.

They watched him until he had disappeared around the opposite side of the butte. When they caught sight of him again Tom had descended to the desert, and was approaching them along the base of the mountain.

"Anything encouraging?" called the Professor.

Parry shook his head.

"Why can't we all go up there and get a breath of fresh air? There must be some breeze on the top of the mountain," suggested Ned.

"No, I couldn't think of it," replied the guide firmly.

"Why not, please?" asked Walter.

"Because you might not come back," replied the guide, with a grim compression of the lips.

Later, upon being pressed by Tad for his reasons, he confided to the lad that there were snakes on the butte. He said he did not care to tell that to the boys, adding that "what they don't know won't hurt them."

Camp was made at dusk, some five miles further on, much to the relief of man and beast, for it had been the most trying day they had experienced.

The boys threw off their sombreros, shaking the dust from their heads. They then removed their clothes, giving them a thorough beating. After a brisk rub down with dry bath towels, the lads announced themselves as ready for supper.

"Our dry spread," Ned Rector called it, for not a drop of anything did they have to drink. They had drained their canteens of what little remained in them.

"It isn't good for one to drink with meals anyway," comforted Stacy. "That's what my uncle's doctor says," he explained, munching his bacon, forcing it down his parched throat.

Chunky was a philosopher, but he was unaware of the fact.

"That is right. Not until an hour and a half after meals," agreed the Professor. "I imagine we shall have to wait longer than that this time."

"Never mind; we'll pull through somehow. We always have," encouraged Tad cheerfully. "We've gotten out of some pretty tight places, and I am sure we'll manage to weather this gale in one way or another."

"Gale? Huh! I wish we had a gale to weather," murmured Walter.

"Providing it was a wet one," added Stacy.

"That's so. Now wouldn't it be fine to have a rainstorm?" agreed Ned, with enthusiasm.

"We could cuddle in our tents and listen to the raindrops patter on the roof," suggested Stacy.

"No; we'd lie down on our backs outside, open our mouths wide——"

"Like a nest of young robins," laughed Tad.

"Yes. Only we'd fill our mouths with water instead of——"

"Boys, boys!" warned the Professor. "I fear you are drifting into questionable dinner topics again."

"Why, we're talking about water, Professor," replied Ned in a tone of innocent surprise. "Surely you do not object to that?"

"Not so long as you confine your remarks to the subject of water. That seems to be our principal need at the present time."

"Speaking of water — —" began Chunky.

"Hold on; is this a story or a joke?" interrupted Ned.

"I heard of a case like ours once," continued the fat boy, without heeding the interruption. "A party of travelers on the desert found themselves without water. In the party was a bookkeeper. He was from the East. Well, they were thinking about dying from thirst. But they didn't. The bookkeeper saved them."

There was silence in the group for a moment.

"I'll be the goat. How did he save them?" asked Ned.

"He had a fountain pen," replied the fat boy sagely.

"Y-e-o-w!" howled the Pony Rider Boys. "Put him out! Put him out!"

# CHAPTER XXI
# OFF ON A DRY TRAIL

"We shall have to divide up our forces to-day, Professor. We'll make a desperate effort to find a water hole," announced Tom Parry.

"What do you propose doing? You mean you're going to let us help you?"

"Yes."

"I'm glad."

"We'll make a big pull to-day. Should we fail to find water there is only one thing left for us to do."

"And that?"

"Leave the burros to shift for themselves. We'll head hack toward the San Antonio Range as fast as the bronchos will carry us. I don't know whether they'll be equal to the strain or not. If they give out we'll have to walk, that's all."

"Impossible!" exclaimed the Professor aghast.

"Nothing's impossible when you're up against it. We'll go through with this, see if we don't. Just keep your nerve, and — —"

"But the boys," protested the Professor.

"Look at them," said Parry. "They're somewhat the worse for wear, it's true, but they're all right, every single one of them. Boys, come over here!"

The lads hastened to obey his summons.

"What is it, Mr. Parry?" questioned Tad.

"We've got to do some real work to-day, boys, and I want you to take a hand."

"We are ready for anything, sir," spoke up Ned.

"Yes, I know that," replied Parry; then went on: "This is the situation. We are without a drop of water. All the water holes that I have been depending upon are dry and there is no certainty that we shall find any that are not in the same condition if we continue on our journey. We can go along for another day, perhaps, so far as we are concerned."

"But the stock won't," interposed Tad.

"No."

"I noticed this morning that some of the ponies were pretty gaunt in the flanks."

"Regular scarecrows. We've got to make an organized search for a tank, and the sooner we begin the better off we'll be — or the worse," added the guide under his breath. "If we fail, we'll ride all night, taking the back trail. We ought to hold out long enough to reach the last water hole we left. Though even that may be dried up by the time we get to it."

"Then you want us to spread out, as it were, and cover all the territory about here?" questioned Tad.

"That's it. You've caught the idea."

Professor Zepplin shook his head.

"I don't like the idea. The boys will be lost."

"They mustn't, that's all," replied the guide, with a firm setting of the lips. "I think we can arrange so they will find their way back to camp all right. Listen! This is my plan. Master Tad will ride west, due west. Master Ned, on the other hand, will proceed east, and I'll go south. Each of us will ride as far as he can until noon. If by then none of us has found any trace of water, we'll all turn about and hurry hack to camp."

"Yes, but how do you expect the boys to find their way hack?" demanded Professor Zepplin.

"I'm coming to that. To begin with, I'm going to splice the ridge poles of the tents together, making a flagpole of them. On this we'll tie a shirt or something, planting the pole on the top of that ridge there. While the boys will be too far away to see it from where they should be by twelve o'clock, they can get near enough, by using their watches as compasses, so they can pick it up. Each one will take a rifle with him, and in the event of finding water he is to remain there, firing off the gun at frequent intervals."

"What'll we be doing here all the time?" interrupted Walter.

"Starting at twelve o'clock, you will begin firing a rifle to help guide the boys in. Fire a shot every five minutes. No chance to get lost at all. Do you think so, Professor?"

"It would seem not. Did I not know from past experiences how easy it is for the boys to get into trouble, I should not hesitate an instant."

"Anyway, we've got to do it. We are at a point where we shall have to take chances. We are taking some as it is. Now, hurry your breakfast. I'll fix up the signal pole while you are doing so, then we'll be off as soon as you have finished."

Both Tad and Ned were enthusiastic and anxious to show themselves capable of taking a man's part in the proposed operations.

"If Chunky only had a fountain pen now all this trouble would be unnecessary," teased Ned as they were hurrying through their breakfast.

The fat boy's soulful eyes held an expression of mild protest, but he made no reply.

The meal finished, Tad and Ned brought out their rifles, which they loaded, taking with them a box of cartridges each. The guide did the same. The flagpole had been planted and from its top fluttered a pair of pink pajamas belonging to the Professor.

"That ought to scare all the coyotes off the desert," commented Ned as the party surveyed the result of the guide's work.

"It will serve still another purpose," grinned the guide. "Some traveler may see it. In that event he'll head for it, thinking it's some one in distress. If he does, you may be able to get a few drops of water from his canteen, providing it's not as empty as our own."

"Oh, how dry I am," whistled Ned softly.

"There doesn't seem to be much probability of our meeting strangers in this desolate place," commented the Professor. "What time do you think we shall see you back? Have you any idea?"

"Somewhere about sunset, in all probability."

"I'd like to go along with Tad," said Stacy.

"Why—no, I think you'd better not," said the Professor.

"Please. I know I shall be able to help him. You do not need two boys in camp with you, Professor."

"Yes; he might as well go along, if he wants to," decided the guide.

"Very well, then. But Walter must remain here."

"Use your old ponies. Do not take the stallions," advised Parry. "If the stallions were to get away from you while you are off on the desert alone it would leave you, and perhaps us as well, in pretty bad shape. And, by the way, Professor, when you begin firing your signals, go to the top of the hill yonder and shoot straight up into the air. The sound will carry further than were you to shoot from here. You've no idea how perplexing this Desert Maze is to those not familiar with it and its tricks."

"I'm learning fast," smiled the Professor. "Furthermore, I am convinced that I shall know all about it if I live long— —"

"Never," answered Parry promptly. "No man ever lived who knew all about the desert. I— —"

"If we rough riders don't get started pretty soon we'll be back before we get started," warned Stacy humorously.

"You're right. We are wasting time. Now, Masters Tad and Ned, you understand what you are to do?"

"We do," answered the boys.

"Follow my directions to the letter. If you do you will keep out of trouble. If you do not, there's no telling what may happen."

"We are to find water. That's what we are going out for," added Tad.

"Exactly. But the instant you hear a gun fired, turn about and ride home. That will mean either that the time's up, or that one or the other of us has found what you are looking for. Keep your eyes clear for signs and for crusts of alkali that may have a water tank under them."

"We'll do our duty, Mr. Parry," answered Tad.

"I know it. Good-bye and good luck!"

The three lads swung their hands in parting salute, as they left the camp at an easy gallop, Tad and Stacy riding side by side, Ned Rector moving off alone. Ascending the rise of ground where the pajamas were drooping listlessly from the top of the signal pole, Tad and Stacy slipped down the opposite side of the hill and disappeared from view.

The two lads were destined to pass through some exciting experiences before they rejoined their companions.

"I hope we don't get lost," said Stacy, apprehensively, as they glided across the desert.

"We mustn't!"

"Yes; but what if we do?" insisted the fat boy.

"It will be because you disobeyed orders, Chunky. You and I have a task to perform, and we're going to do it like men. The lives of our companions may depend upon our own efforts—yours and mine."

"I can't see the Professor's pajamas," insisted Chunky. "I believe we are lost already, Tad."

"Then we'll stay lost," answered Tad shortly.

# CHAPTER XXII
# IN THE HERMIT'S CAVE

The conviction that they did not know where they were grew upon Stacy as they proceeded. Not that Stacy cared particularly whether they were lost or not, but it gave him something to talk about.

"Don't talk so much, Chunky," begged Tad, after they had gone on some distance. "You should keep your eyes out for signs."

"What kind of signs?"

"Water signs. Come, be serious for a little while. You can have all the sport you want when we get back. I think, Chunky, that we can both work to better advantage if we separate— —"

"What, you want to get rid of me so soon?"

"No, no! Listen! You ride off there to the right, say half a mile. Keep within sight of me all the time, and watch carefully for what we are in search of. We shall be able to do twice as effective work in that way."

"I see. I guess that would be a good idea. Got anything to eat in your pocket?"

"Some dry bread. I'll divide with you. You should have brought something."

The fat boy, well satisfied now, rode away to the north, munching the dry food that Tad had given him. So long as Chunky had plenty to eat, nothing else mattered.

Tad soon espied what appeared to him to be a cloud on the horizon ahead. After a time he discovered that it was a range of irregular buttes. On some of them he eventually made out what looked like scattering trees. Tad increased the speed of his pony as much as he thought the animal would stand. If there were trees, there surely should be water as well, he reasoned. After a time he succeeded in attracting the attention of Stacy, whom he motioned to him.

The fat boy put spurs to his mount, racing along one side of the triangle, heading for the range, for which he observed that Tad was riding. It was now a test of speed to see which one should get there first. Tad having the shorter distance to travel, made the mark ahead of his companion, though with little to spare.

"You started before I knew what you were up to," laughed Stacy. "I can beat you on an even start."

"Haven't any doubt of it, Chunky. But let's see what's to be found here. It looks promising. You hold the horses while I climb up among the rocks."

"There's a man up there!" exclaimed Stacy. "What's he doing? I wonder if he's a hermit? Looks as if he might be."

"I'll find out. If some one is living here, there's water," cried Tad triumphantly, leaping from his saddle and tossing the bridle reins to his companion.

The lad ran lightly up the rocks toward the point where he saw the stranger standing, observing them suspiciously. As he drew nearer to the figure, Tad felt some apprehension. The man was thin and gaunt, a heavy growth of beard covering his face so completely as to hide everything except the nose and eyes.

"I believe he's crazy," muttered the lad, when he got near enough to note the strange expression in the fellow's eyes. As yet, the man had not spoken a word.

"How do you do, sir!" greeted the boy.

The hermit, for such he proved to be, grunted an unintelligible reply.

"We are looking for water. My friends are camped off yonder, a dozen miles or more, and our water is all gone. Please tell me where I can find some?"

"Got money?"

"Yes, yes, I've got money. I will pay you for your trouble if that is what you want. Let me have a drink first and take some to my companion; then I will do whatever you wish in the way of paying," begged the lad.

The hermit eyed him with a steady, disconcerting gaze that gave Tad a creepy feeling up and down his spine.

"You want water?"

"Yes, yes."

A moment's hesitation, then the hermit grasped Tad by the arm and strode rapidly back among the rocks. Pushing aside a growth of tangled vines he stooped to enable him to enter the opening that was revealed, dragging Tad in after him.

**The Hermit Grasped Tad by the Arm.**

"See here, where are you taking me?" demanded the lad, pulling back instinctively from the dark opening.

The hermit made no reply, but tightening his grip, which was of vise-like firmness, jerked the boy into the center of the chamber. Tad observed by the single ray of light that penetrated the place through the mat of vines at the entrance that they were in a cave.

"You want water?" snapped the hermit.

"Yes, I do want water more than anything else in the world at this minute, but there is no necessity for dragging me to it. I can walk."

"Water in there," answered the hermit, thrusting Tad into a dark recess. No sooner had he done so than the lad heard a heavy wooden door slammed shut and a bar thrown across it from the outside.

Tad, instantly realizing that he was being shut in, threw himself against the barrier with all his strength. But he might as well have tried to break through the rocks which walled him in on the other three sides. He shouted at the top of his voice, hoping that Chunky might, perchance, hear him and come to his rescue. Chunky could use the rifle that hung in the holster on Tad's saddle and intimidate the hermit if he understood Tad's predicament.

At that instant the lad's ears caught the faint trickle of water. The sound stirred him to sudden action. "Where was it?" he asked himself, his hands groping over the rocks about him.

"Here it is!" he cried exultingly.

What he had found was a tiny stream that was creeping down the side of the rocks. Tad pressed his lips against the cool stones, enabling him to lick a few drops of the precious fluid into his parched mouth. Never had anything tasted so refreshing to him.

"A-h-h-h-h!" gasped the boy, taking a fresh breath preparatory to another draught. "It's almost worth being made a prisoner for this. I'll bet Chunky would wish to be in here if he knew. And I almost wish he were."

As if in answer to his expressed wish, the door was suddenly pushed inward, a heavy body was hurled in, landing in a heap on the rocky floor.

The door slammed shut and the bar once more fell into place.

For the moment Tad could not determine what had happened.

"I—I fell in," moaned a voice from the heap.

"Chunky!" cried Tad. "How did you get in here?"

"I—just dropped in," wailed the fat boy.

"Get up! Don't be a baby! Come here and have a drink of water— —"

"Water? Water?" fairly shouted Stacy, leaping to his feet, bumping against a rock in his haste. "Where? Where?"

"Here. Put your lips against the rock right here. There, you have it. Does it taste good?"

"U-m-m-m."

"Now, you've had enough for the moment. Tell me how you got here? How did you happen to come up?" questioned Tad.

"The—the wild man—say, Tad, he looks like a monkey, doesn't he?"

"I hadn't thought of it in that light. I guess you're right, though, Chunky."

"Well, he went out on the rocks and motioned to me. I told him I couldn't leave the ponies. He said you wanted me right away, and he came down to help me stake the ponies. He was awful kind," mused Stacy, as if talking to himself.

"Go on," urged Tad. "We've got to think about what's going to become of us."

"That's all. He just led me up here. Said you were inside getting water. Then—then he threw me in. Think I hurt the floor when I hit it, Tad?"

"I guess not quite so bad as that," laughed the lad. "I want you to strike a match while I look around the place."

Stacy did so, taking his time about it. By the dim light thus made, they discovered a little pool of water in a far corner of the chamber, where the trickling stream had found it's way. With their drinking cups, which, with their canteens, the boys always carried, they dipped the pool almost dry, filling their canteens with the cool, refreshing water, after having first fully satisfied their thirst.

"Got anything to eat?" questioned Stacy, his thoughts turning to food.

"Yes, and I'm going to keep it," answered Tad promptly.

"That's mean."

"See here, Chunky. We are prisoners. We don't know when or how we are going to get out. I have a few crusts of bread left and I propose to keep them, because we may find ourselves starving later on. You'll be glad then that I saved the bread. What do you think the hermit intends to do? Did he say anything that gave you any clue?"

"Nope."

"We'll wait a while and if he does not let us out, we'll have to find a way for ourselves."

For a time they made the best of their situation, Stacy grumbling now and then, Tad bright and cheery, though in his heart he felt far from cheerful.

"I'm going to try to break the door down," announced Tad finally, after listening intently. "I can't hear anything. I believe the hermit has gone away and left us. Get up here beside me. Take hold of my hand and we'll rush it together."

They did so, throwing their combined weight against the door.

"Ouch!" yelled Stacy.

"Never mind, try it again," encouraged Tad, laughing in spite of himself.

Once more they hurled themselves on the obstruction. It resisted all their efforts. Tad lighted a match, examining the door carefully. The light revealed a heap of blankets in a corner of the chamber, where the old hermit slept.

"Must be his bedroom," decided Chunky.

"We've got to try something else," announced Tad. "Got your knife!"

"Yes."

"Out with it. We're going to whittle. Lucky for us that our knives are big and sharp. Hold a match while I mark out the spot we're going to try to cut out."

Tad had sounded the door with his fist until he found the place where the bar on the other side held it. He also discovered sockets for an inner bar, by which the hermit probably locked himself in at night. Then he began cutting.

"You start in here and keep to your side so you don't cut my hands," the lad directed.

The crunching sound of their knives began immediately, the work going on more slowly in the darkness than would have been the case had they had light. Now and then the lads would pause to listen. Not a sound penetrated to their prison. Tad thought this very strange, unless perhaps the hermit might be lying in wait to fall upon them in case they did succeed in freeing themselves.

"Say, Tad."

"Well?"

"I've got an idea." Chunky's knife had been silent for a few moments.

"What is it?"

"Let's burn down the old door."

"How!"

"I'll show you."

Stacy scraped industriously for a time, then lighting a match applied it to the spot on which he had been working. The splinters caught fire burned up briskly then went out. Stacy repeated the process with a similar result.

"I guess that will help a little," decided Tad, running his fingers over the spot.

"Just like singeing the pin feathers off an old hen—the feathers burn, but the hen doesn't," grumbled Stacy.

"Whew! the smoke's getting thick in here. We've got to stop the burning or we'll suffocate," warned Tad. "Wish I had an ax. I'd make short work of the old door."

They then began working with a grim determination, Stacy ceasing his joking. At last a tiny ray of light showed through the heavy door.

"Hurrah!" shouted Tad. "I see daylight."

"Then give me some bread. I'm hungry."

"Not yet. We're not out of our prison," laughed Tad. "Keep cutting. It will take all of an hour to make an opening large enough for me to get my hand through——"

"I got my finger through," cried Stacy triumphantly. "Ouch!" he yelled as a club of some sort was brought against the door on the outside with terrific force, bruising the end of the lad's finger.

"The hermit is out there waiting for us!" gasped Tad, with sinking heart.

# CHAPTER XXIII
## LOST IN THE DESERT MAZE

A rifle shot sounded from the camp of the Pony Rider Boys. At regular intervals shot followed shot.

It was the warning signal agreed upon to notify the others that water had been found. Ned Rector had ridden into camp with the joyful tidings that he had discovered a water tank about three miles to the eastward. Immediately Walter sprang for his rifle, and running to the top of the little hill began shooting into the air. Ned, in the meantime, not waiting for the return of the others, had fetched the water-bags from the burros, and started off at a rapid pace to bring back water for the stock. His canteen he left for Professor Zepplin and Walter.

"It's horrible stuff, but it is water," breathed the Professor as he swallowed the brown alkali fluid. "If ever I get a drink of real water again, I know I shall be able to appreciate it."

In the meantime Walter's rifle was booming its warning over the desert maze.

Two hours later, Tom Parry, hot, dusty and well-nigh spent, rode into camp with the steam rising from his pony in a thin, vaporous cloud.

"Have you found it?" he called hoarsely.

"Yes; Ned's found a water hole," the Professor informed him.

"Give me a drink, quick. The alkali's cutting furrows in my throat," he begged. "Never got such a hold of me before."

The Professor pressed his canteen to the guide's lips, and Parry drank eagerly. A few moments later he pulled himself together sharply.

"I'm going to take the stock out to the water hole," he announced, starting the burros off across the desert. "I'll water the stallions when I return."

"You had better let me attend to that," protested the Professor. "You're in no shape to go out in the sun again."

"That's all right, Professor. But tell me how I am going to get out of the sun?" begged Parry, with a grim smile.

"The tent— —"

"Hotter than the sun. No, I guess I can stand it if those boys are able to. By the way, have you seen anything of the other two?"

"I'll ascertain if Walter has discovered them yet."

Walter's straining eyes had failed to make out Tad and Stacy, however, so the Professor bade him continue firing his rifle. This was a pleasant occupation for Walter, for, like his companions, next to a pony he loved a gun.

Ned had returned with the water-bags, and Parry had finished watering the stock. It was now near sunset.

"No signs yet?" questioned the guide, joining Walter on the knoll.

"Not a thing."

"That doesn't seem right. Stop your firing and come get some supper. We must eat and put ourselves in shape or we'll be good for nothing. Did those boys take any food with them?"

"I think I saw Tad stowing something in his pockets before he started. I'm sure I did," spoke up Ned Rector.

"There's a lad who knows his business," approved Parry, moving toward the camp with Walter.

"Why have you discontinued the shooting?" demanded the Professor in surprise.

"To eat. Half an hour's intermission will make little difference. If the lads are on their way, we'll be able to call them in before it gets dark. If not, then I shall go out to look for them. They're all right. I think you need feel no concern over them."

"Must have gone a long way," spoke up Ned.

"Yes, they undoubtedly followed orders."

"And perhaps exceeded them," added the Professor.

It was a real supper that they sat down to that evening, with hot coffee, fried bacon and other good things, and the party would have been a jolly one had Tad and Stacy been on hand to participate in it.

Walter hurried through his meal, then took his position on the hill once more, where he renewed his signaling with the rifle.

All at once he uttered a shout, following it with a quick volley of six shots, thus emptying his magazine.

"Do you see them!" called Parry, hastening over to the knoll, and joining Walter.

"I think I see a cloud of dust approaching over the desert," he made reply.

"Where?"

Walter pointed with his rifle.

"Yes, that's the boys, I guess. Nothing but a broncho could kick up the alkali like that. I'll go back and have their supper ready. You keep on shooting. The light is growing fainter and they won't be able to find their way in otherwise."

"Is it the boys?" called the Professor, as they saw Parry hastening toward them.

"I think so. Put the coffee on, Master Ned. They'll want to boil the alkali out of their systems as soon as they get here."

"That's the time Tad Butler got left," chuckled Ned Rector. "He's always been around when there was any glory coming. But when it comes to finding water where there isn't any, I guess they can't beat Ned Rector."

"What's that boy shooting so rapidly for?" asked Parry.

"He's excited about something," answered Ned. "He's dancing around as if he's suddenly gone crazy. What's that? He's calling and motioning to us. Guess he wants you, Mr. Parry."

"What is it!" called the guide, making a megaphone of his hands.

Unable to make out what it was that Walter was shouting to him, Tom Parry deserted the camp-fire, where he was assisting to get the second supper, and hastened to the knoll.

"What's the trouble, my lad?"

"Come and see. I want you to take a look at that pony. He's tearing across the desert as if something were chasing him. But I can't make out anyone on his back."

"The light is weak and he's throwing a lot of dust. Of course there's some one his back, and there must be two horses."

The guide shaded his hands, gazing off across the plain.

"What—what——" he stammered.

"Wasn't I right, Mr. Parry?"

"That's very strange. I don't understand it at all."

"That's what I thought."

"There's only one pony and he's riderless," exclaimed Tom Parry. "I'm afraid something has happened. It may not be one of our ponies, however. We'll know in a few minutes."

The running animal was drawing steadily nearer the camp. Those over by the camp-fire were busy getting the meal ready for the two missing lads. The pony reached the foot of the knoll. Observing Parry and Walter there, the little animal shied, making a wide detour, and finally galloping up to the camp.

Walter and the guide hurried down.

"Hello!" cried the Professor, as he saw the horse dash in. "What does this mean!"

"Why, it's Tad's pony!" exclaimed Ned in amazement.

"Is that Master Tad's mount?" called the guide as he approached them on the run.

"Yes. Do you think there's anything wrong?" questioned Ned.

"Looks that way. Don't let him get away. I want to look the critter over. Perhaps we may learn something."

Ned caught the pony without difficulty, and led it to the guide. Parry went all over the animal, even going through the saddlebags.

"The rifle and the rope are missing. Everything else seems to be in order," he announced.

"Then I'll guarantee that Tad's all right," spoke up Ned.

"That's what I think," agreed Walter. "He's taken his gun and rope up into some mountain or other and while he was away the pony got away and started for home."

"Is that your opinion, Mr. Parry?" questioned the Professor.

"What's the use in offering any opinions? I don't know. But I'm going to find out. Let's see. We have a new moon to-night. I've got about two hours before it goes down. I want you all to remain right here in camp until I return. Even if it's until to-morrow. I'm going out to look for the boys."

With that Parry hastily filled his canteen, slung one of the bags of water over the back of his pony, and springing into the saddle dashed away, following the trail that the returning broncho had left.

# CHAPTER XXIV
# CONCLUSION

"No use trying to go any further to-night, Chunky."

"Where'll we stay, then?"

"Right here, I guess," answered Tad. "It's as good a place as we'll find."

But to understand this, we must take up the fortunes of Tad and Stacy, whom we left imprisoned in the hermit's cave.

After waiting for a full hour in the cave, following the hermit's blow on the door, the lads not having heard anything further of him, had renewed their whittling. After long and arduous effort they had succeeded in making an opening in the wood sufficiently large to enable Tad to push his hand through.

Before doing so, however, he made reasonably sure that the hermit was not standing there with a club ready to bring it down with crushing force.

Being satisfied on this point, Tad thrust a hand through. His upturned hand had grasped the bar that held the door in place. Pushing upward with all his strength he felt the bar give.

Stacy, with ready resourcefulness, began forcing up on Tad's elbow. In a moment more they had the satisfaction of hearing the bar clatter to the rocks. Yet one end of it had stuck in its socket, still holding the barrier in place.

They tried their former tactics. Backing off, both lads rushed at the heavy door. It gave way with a suddenness that they had not expected. The boys tumbled out, each landing on his head and shoulders, then toppling over to his back.

There was a lively scramble. They were up in a twinkling, fully expecting to find the hermit standing over them. To their surprise, they found themselves entirely alone. To their further surprise, neither of their ponies was in sight when they stepped out on the rocks.

Upon examining the hoof prints a few minutes later they discovered that one animal had set off on the back trail, while the other had apparently gone in the opposite direction.

After a brief consultation they decided that they must start back on foot. Without a moment's hesitation, the lads, laying their course by Tad's watch, started pluckily toward camp, many miles away.

After a few hours night overtook them. They still had the moon, however, and by its light they trudged along for two more weary hours. Then the moon's light left them and Tad decided that it were worse than useless to continue.

Absolute darkness had settled over the Desert Maze as the boys dropped down, footsore and weary after their long tramp in the stifling heat.

"Got anything to eat?" asked Stacy.

"That I have, and a canteen of water besides. We have a lot to be thankful for yet, Chunky. Haven't we?"

"I'll tell you after I try the bread," answered the fat boy.

Tad laughed merrily.

"Always a humorist, aren't you?"

"Except when I fall in somewhere," replied Stacy.

"How does the bread go?"

"Fine!"

"Aren't you glad you didn't eat it up back there in the hermit's cave?"

"Oh, I dunno. If I'd eaten it then, I wouldn't have to eat it now."

"Oh, Chunky, you're hopeless. I shall have to give you up——"

"What do you think has become of those ponies?" interrupted the fat boy.

"Guess they must have gotten away and gone home—at least one of them," answered Tad.

"Wrong."

"Why?"

"One went one way and the other another, didn't he?"

"Yes. What of that?"

"If they'd gotten away they'd both traveled together. One of them was ridden away and I'm thinking the hermit was on his back. I'll bet he carried my broncho off."

"You mean you think your broncho carried him off?" laughed Tad. "I didn't give you credit for so much sense, Chunky. I guess you are right at that. The ponies surely would have left together. Seems to be our luck to lose horses. Guess my gun has gone, too, but I picked up the rope back by the mountain."

"Glad I didn't bring my rifle along," chuckled Stacy. "I'll bet I'd be throwing good-bye kisses after it now if I had."

"I don't understand what that old man meant by making us prisoners unless it was that he wanted a horse to get out of the Desert Maze. If that was his reason, I don't blame him," laughed Tad. "Mr. Parry did us a real service when he advised us to leave our stallions back in camp. They surely would have been gone by this time, and we never could have caught them again."

"Yes; I can see Satan legging it for the hills," replied Stacy. "Legging it is his strong point."

They had finished their slender meal by this time and drunk their fill of water from the canteens. As a result, they felt better than they had felt at any time during the past three days.

"We have a long, hot walk ahead of us to-morrow, unless they come out to look for us, Chunky," averred Tad.

"Yes. And I love to walk," replied Stacy, with droll humor. "Especially when the sun is one hundred and fifty in the shade, or where the shade ought to be. If ever I come down in this baked country again, I'm going to bring that sweet apple tree out of uncle's orchard, even if I have to drag it all over the desert with me."

"Think we'd better make our beds and turn in?" suggested Tad.

"I guess. I'll take a drink of water first; then I'm ready."

In a few moments the plucky lads had stretched out on the still hot ground, without feeling the least fear. They were too self-reliant to feel any fear, and they had passed so many nights in the open that the mysterious darkness of the outside world held no terrors for them. They knew there was nothing to harm them.

Tad was beginning to doze off when Stacy nudged him in the ribs.

"What is it?" asked Tad sharply.

"I think the girl forgot to put a fresh pillow case on my pillow today. The pillow feels awful rough."

"Oh, go to sleep. Dream all the funny things you wish to, but don't bother me till daylight."

From that moment until long past midnight the boys slept soundly, neither having moved since he lay down for his night's rest. Even when the coyotes began to howl, off on the desert, the lads merely stirred, only half conscious of what the sound meant. But when the howls gradually drew nearer, Chunky cautiously opened one eye. The night was so dark that he could not see anything about him.

The beasts drew nearer. Tad was awake now.

"Keep still, don't scare them until I give the word," he said in answer to Stacy's poke.

Emboldened by the quietness, the coyotes kept creeping closer and closer, their mournful howls increasing in volume every minute. All at once Tad reached down for his rope. He lay still for a few minutes until satisfied that the animals had not observed his movement. Suddenly the great loop shot from his hand.

A quick, violent tug at the other end, a wild, frightened howl from the cowardly beasts, and all but one, with tails between their legs, fled over the desert.

"I've got one, Chunky," yelled Tad. "Quick! Help me here, or he'll get away!"

It required all the strength of the two boys to hold the animal that Tad had roped in the dark. Gradually they shortened up on the rope, Tad standing in front of his companion until he felt the animal dangerously near. Then he let out a swift kick. By good luck, it laid the coyote flat.

Tad was upon the beast before, in its half-dazed condition, it could rise. Together they tied the animal's feet, its jaws snapping at them viciously before their task was completed.

There was no more sleep for the lads that night. They feared the coyote would gnaw the rope in two, if left alone. All during the night the boys were obliged continually to jerk on the line about its neck to keep the beast from doing this very thing.

Morning came at last. Making a harness from a piece of the rope, they bound up one of the animal's forefeet, just as Bud Stevens had done with wild horses. Then they released the hind feet. Mr. Coyote hopped about like a rabbit for a time, snarling and snapping, to their keen delight. They felt no fear of him, though Mr. Coyote had several times expressed a willingness to fight his captors.

After eating their remaining crumbs of bread, the boys decided to move on. Tad, believing that he knew the direction to follow, did not wait for the sun to rise. Yet, although they were not aware of the fact, they already had strayed far from the trail.

"I'm afraid the coyote is going to be a drag on us, much as I should like to take him along," said Tad.

Stacy begged to keep the animal, and Tad decided to try it. The next question was, how to move it. It was finally decided that one boy should lead the coyote while the other prodded it from the rear when the animal lagged.

At noon they halted to rest, draining the last drop from their canteens. Then they started on again, suffering more and more from the heat as they proceeded. About the middle of the afternoon Tad halted, gazing helplessly about him.

"Chunky, we're lost in the Desert Maze. I don't know where I am any more than if I were in the middle of an ocean. I'm pretty nearly exhausted, too."

"So's the coyote," comforted Stacy.

"But we've got to keep on going. My watch is missing. I must have lost it where we slept last night. I can only guess at the direction we ought to take. Have you any idea where we are?"

Stacy gazed at the sky meditatively.

"On a rough guess, I should say we were on the Nevada Desert."

"Oh, come on! Come on!"

Still clinging to the angry coyote, the lads took up their weary tramp. The baking alkali burned their feet almost to the blistering point; the burning, withering heat made their heads whirl; the desert began to perform strange antics, while the halo that they had seen a few days before again appeared before them, first whirling like a giant pin wheel, then oscillating in a way that made them giddy.

"Chunky, I can't stand this any longer," cried Tad, suddenly sinking to the ground. "I'm ashamed of myself to give way like this."

Stacy moved around to the sunny side of his companion, placing his own body where it would shade Tad's head from the sun. The fat boy took off his sombrero, unheeding the burning rays that were beating down on his own head, and began to fan Tad with the hat.

"I don't believe I can go any further, Chunky. You are still in fairly good shape and you'll be able to make the camp if you go on. Leave me and make a try for it."

"You—you want me to go on without you? Want me to leave you here to—Say, Tad, do you think I'm that kind of a coyote? I'd thrash you for that if you weren't already properly done up. You'll feel better when night comes and your head gets cooled off. In the morning we'll make another attempt to get out of the Desert Maze. You lie still, now."

Thus admonished, Tad closed his eyes. At last the sun went down, and with its passing, came a breath of refreshing air. They inhaled long and deeply of it. After a little, Stacy got up.

"Where you going?" demanded Tad, opening his bloodshot eyes.

"Going to tie up my dog, then go to bed."

Five minutes later both were sleeping the sleep that comes from utter exhaustion of mind and body.

Stacy awakened first, his eyes opening on the burning blue above him. After a few moments he rolled over on his stomach to gaze at the coyote. Instantly something else attracted his attention. What he saw was a crossed stick on a standard. The whole resembled a cross, standing barely six inches above the ground.

The lad eyed the strange object inquiringly, then wriggled over toward it.

"Maybe there's water here. I'll see," he muttered. Stacy began digging industriously with knife and hands.

After a time the knife struck some hard substance. This, upon further digging, proved to be a bottle. The boy pulled his find out quickly.

"There's a piece of paper in it," he exclaimed in surprise. "Guess somebody must have thrown it off a sinking desert schooner."

Stacy drew the paper from the bottle.

"'To the lost on the Desert Maze,'" he read "That's me and the coyote. 'Water ten paces to the east. Grass Peak fifteen miles to the east. Belted Range about eighteen miles west. Cross piece on stick, points due east and west. A Traveler.'"

With a sharp glance at his sleeping companion, Stacy tramped off ten paces. There being no sign of water, the lad began stamping about with his heels. Suddenly the alkali crust gave way beneath him. One leg went through. He felt it plunge into water.

"Y-e-o-w!" howled Stacy.

Tad Butler scrambled to his feet, rubbing his eyes.

"Water! Water! Water! I fell in!" shrieked the fat boy, dancing about joyously. "I've found a key to the Desert Maze, and I've unlocked one blind desert alley with my foot."

The lads drank and drank of the villainous, brown fluid. Then, after having laved their faces and filled the canteens, they set out on their journey. Grass Peak was the hill from which the Professor's pajamas had been unfurled to the idle desert breeze.

Twilight was descending when two gaunt-eyed, hollow-cheeked lads, each with an arm thrown about the other's waist for support, were described, staggering across the Desert Maze. Behind then, at the end of a lariat, slouched a disconsolate, cowardly coyote.

A great shout went up from the camp of the Pony Riders.

They dashed out to meet their exhausted companions. Hoisting the two boys to their shoulders, they carried them triumphantly to camp.

Tom Parry, the guide, had been thrown by his pony stepping through a crust on the alkali, and had lain all night on the desert. Next day he had staggered back to camp, where he found his pony, and after a few hours' rest had taken up his fruitless search again.

Stacy's pony in the meantime had come in. The boys never knew how the animals got away, though from the fact that Tad's rifle was missing, it was believed that the hermit had ridden the pony off, turning it adrift later.

But the brave lads had found their way through the Desert Maze to camp, having passed through hardships and perils that would have daunted stronger and more experienced desert travelers.

Next morning the Pony Rider Boys struck their tents and broke camp. A few days later they crossed the line into California, where, after loading their stock and equipment into a large stock car, they started for the East.

Yet, though their summer vacation was rapidly drawing to a close, the Pony Rider Boys had not seen the end of their thrilling adventures. Another exciting trip lay before them; one which was destined to linger in memory for many years to come. The story of this, the end of the Silver Trail, will be related in a following volume entitled, "THE PONY RIDER BOYS IN NEW MEXICO."

## THE END